Taming *the* Flame

Secrets for Hot-and-Quick Grilling and Low-and-Slow BBQ

Special edition created for

Elizabeth Karmel

Wiley Publishing, Inc.

This booklet is printed on acid-free paper. ∞
Adapted from *Taming the Flame: Secrets for Hot-and-Quick Grilling and Low-and-Slow BBQ.*
Copyright © 2005 by Elizabeth A. Karmel. All rights reserved
Cover photographs and photographs on pages iv, vi, and 6, © Christopher Hirsheimer.
All other photos courtesy of © Vacu Vin, Inc.
Published by John Wiley & Sons, Inc., Hoboken, New Jersey.

No part of this publication may be reproduced, stored in a retrieval system, or transmitted in any form or by any means, electronic, mechanical, photocopying, recording, scanning, or otherwise, except as permitted under Section 107 or 108 of the 1976 United States Copyright Act, without either the prior written permission of the Publisher, or authorization through payment of the appropriate per-copy fee to the Copyright Clearance Center, 222 Rosewood Drive, Danvers, MA 01923, (978) 750-8400, fax (978) 646-8600, or on the web at www.copyright.com.

Requests to the Publisher for permission should be addressed to the Permissions Department, John Wiley & Sons, Inc., 111 River Street, Hoboken, NJ 07030, (201) 748-6011, fax (201) 748-6008, or online at http://www.wiley.com/go/permission.

Limit of Liability/Disclaimer of Warranty: While the publisher and the author have used their best efforts in preparing this book, they make no representations or warranties with respect to the accuracy or completeness of the contents of this book and specifically disclaim any implied warranties of merchantability or fitness for a particular purpose. No warranty may be created or extended by sales representatives or written sales materials. The advice and strategies contained herein may not be suitable for your situation. You should consult with a professional where appropriate. Neither the publisher nor the author shall be liable for any loss of profit or any other commercial damages, including but not limited to special, incidental, consequential, or other damages.

For general information about our other products and services, please contact our Customer Care Department within the United States at (800) 762-2974, outside the United States at (317) 572-3993 or fax (317) 572-4002.

Wiley also publishes its books in a variety of electronic formats. Some content that appears in print may not be available in electronic books. For more information about Wiley products, visit our web site at www.wiley.com.

ISBN-13 978-0-470-04837-5 (pbk.)
ISBN-10 0-470-04837-9 (pbk.)

Printed in the Netherlands
10 9 8 7 6 5 4 3 2

Special Vacu Vin Edition

Contents

Introduction   *v*

NOTE FROM THE MANUFACTURER: VACU VIN TIPS AND USAGE INFORMATION   1

GRILLING METHODS 101   2
Seasoning the Food   2
Big, Bold Flavor Enhancers   3

SELECT RECIPES FROM
Taming the Flame   6
Chicken   7
Duck   10
Beef   11
Pork   17
Lamb   21
Fish   23
Shellfish   26
Vegetables   29
Ribs   31
Basic Brine and Simple Marinades   35

BE WINE SMART: SUGGESTIONS FROM VACU VIN   36

Index   *39*

Introduction

A few years ago I received the Vacu Vin Instant Marinater as a gift. It sat in my kitchen unused until one night when I was going to an impromptu cookout with some college friends. The hostess had purchased salmon for everyone and requested that I grill it at the party. As I was putting my "secret" ingredients (basically anything in my fridge that I could throw together to make a marinade) into my bag, I picked up the Instant Marinater and thought that tonight was a great night to test it out and see what the collective opinion of my old friends would be—I knew they would tell me the truth!

Well, the result was so dramatic that I wrote my improvised recipe down and even told my Vacu Vin story in the headnote when I published the recipe in my cookbook, *Taming the Flame*. I wrote, "the Marinater literally forced the flavor into the fish in only five minutes and the lemon zest tasted fresh, sparkling, and bright—as if I just zested it—even after grilling for 20 minutes." To this day, I use the recipe (Grilled Fish with a Ginger-Soy-Citrus Marinade, page 23) and the Instant Marinater for salmon, sea bass, snapper, or any other fish that I want to liven up with the sharp, clean flavors of ginger, lemon, and soy.

The Instant Marinater was designed by the company that invented the original Vacuum Wine Saver—now used by more than 25 million wine drinkers around the world. The well-known Vacu Vin Wine Saver rescues opened bottles of wine from the perils of oxidizing—a process that ruins the flavor of wine—by eliminating the oxygen inside the bottle and creating a vacuum seal.

With the Instant Marinater, Vacu Vin has turned the tables of home cooks by reducing the oxygen in a marinating environment to *lock in* the flavor. The vacuum process of the Instant Marinater removes the air from the container and the food, allowing the marinade to take the place of the air and *force* all the flavors of the marinade into the food.

It may sound complicated, but it is really a very simple concept: Remember that all food naturally has air in it, and the vacuum process removes that air when it is pumped out of the container, sealing the lid. This process allows the marinade to take up the space where the air used to be. When the vacuum is released, the food is resealed with the marinade *locked in* to the empty pockets that the air used to take up—allowing the marinade to go beyond just the surface of the food and sealing in the flavor.

This is why the marinating is instantaneous. You don't need to let it soak for a long period of time because the flavor is "locked in" the food when the vacuum seal is broken. For more intense marinating, you may repeat the vacuum process a few more times.

So, now that you know the Instant Marinater works, and why it works, use these delicious grilling recipes to try it yourself at home. They're from my 368-page cookbook, *Taming the Flame*, and include some of my favorite marinade-based recipes as well as a few classics to add to your backyard repertoire. And once you've tried a few of my recipes, let your imagination be your guide and make up a marinade of your own. Just remember that every marinade must have an acid (citrus juice, wine, vinegar, etc.), a base (oil, mayonnaise, pesto, etc.), and flavoring agents!

My fifteen-year (and growing strong) love affair with outdoor cooking makes me feel like the luckiest girl in the world. It is the most generous and congenial of the cooking arts, as everyone has a favorite story to tell or a prize-winning recipe to share. My book, *Taming the Flame*, celebrates many of my fabulous fiery experiences on the barbecue trail as well as the close friendships that are sparked by a love of live-fire cooking—grilling or barbecue.

I can't think of a better way to spend all day every day.

Grill away!

Elizabeth

Author of *Taming the Flame: Secrets for Hot-and-Quick Grilling and Low-and-Slow BBQ*, creator of www.GirlsattheGrill.com, and Grill Friends™ Tools and Ceramics

P.S. Outdoor cooking is casual and fun, not stuffy or pretentious, and that is how I wrote my book, casually, with a lot of colloquialisms and humor, and also real-world tips and suggestions. Think of me as a *grill friend* in the backyard with you, guiding you along. If your questions aren't answered here, check out my book, and feel free to e-mail me at Elizabeth@GirlsattheGrill.com.

Note *from the Manufacturer:*
Vacu Vin Tips *and* Usage
Information

Congratulations! You have just purchased one of the most helpful kitchen tools in preparing poultry, meat, fish, vegetables, and more.

The Instant Marinater is ideal for marinating many types of foods. Just follow these easy steps for successful marinating in the Vacu Vin Instant Marinater:

1. Place food to be marinated inside the marinater. Foods can be stacked on top of each other, and this marinater can easily accommodate several steaks, chops, chicken breasts or thighs, hamburgers, many different kinds of fish, shellfish, and an array of vegetables. We suggest you marinate each food type separately and not combine them.

2. Simply create your marinade (see page 4 for ideas) and pour it over the food to be marinated. Seasoning may also be added at this time.

3. Secure lid to the top of the marinating dish and place pump over the stopper and begin to remove the air by moving the pump handle up and down while holding the pump base over the stopper. When you begin to feel some resistance, you should stop pumping. This pumping action eliminates air and opens the pores of the meat, fish, or other food being marinated. Once the lid is secure, you can rotate the marinating dish several times to ensure

Vacu Vin Instant Marinater

that your marinade has come in contact with all of your food.

4. In about five minutes, the marinade will easily penetrate into the pores of your food and give it a wonderful flavor. Cooking can begin immediately. If you plan to wait several hours before cooking, we suggest you put the prepared food and the Instant Marinater in the refrigerator. *Never store warm food in the Instant Marinater under vacuum.*

5. Ideal for working families who don't have much time to spend in the kitchen and weekend chefs who want to prepare the perfect mouthwatering entrée. Great for foods to be cooked on the grill, broiled, or baked.

6. Cleanup is easy: Simply dispose of the excess marinade and wash. Place the Instant Marinater on the top rack of the dishwasher for easy cleaning.

All of the recipes in this book call for a specific grilling method. If you are unsure of what a "grilling method" means in a recipe, refer to the brief guideline below before you begin. For more information, check out *Taming the Flame* or www.GirlsattheGrill.com.

Grilling Method: Direct, Indirect, and Combo

Direct Grilling means that the food is set directly over the heat source—similar to broiling in your oven. My general rule of thumb is to cook food using this method if it takes less than 20 minutes to cook.

Indirect Grilling means that the heat is on either side of the food and the burners are turned off under the food. Use this method if the food takes more than 20 minutes to cook.

Combo Grilling means that you sear the food over direct heat (perhaps to sear a whole tenderloin or a thick steak) before moving it to indirect heat to finish the cooking process. This technique works well for everything from chops to whole tenderloins and even slices of hard squash and potatoes. It is a time-honored and well-respected tradition and the outdoor grill version of the way most restaurant chefs cook almost everything—searing on the stove and finishing the dish in the oven.

Heat Temperature

I've put together the following temperature chart for indirect grilling, to give you an idea of what temperature I have in mind when I call for high, medium, and low. Direct grilling temperatures will be slightly higher since all of the burners are turned on.

The temperature correlations between low, medium, and high are based on preheating your gas grill for 10 minutes with all burners turned to high. These temperatures are the same for charcoal briquettes that have burned down and are covered with a white-gray ash (after 25 to 30 minutes).

High	425–500°F
Medium-High	375–425°F
Medium	325–375°F
Medium-Low	300–325°F
Low	275–300°F

Note: These are my definitions as there are no industry standards that I know of.

Seasoning the Food

Season to taste, adjust seasonings, salt and pepper to taste. These phrases are used over and over again on cooking shows, in magazines, and in cookbooks. What do these statements really mean to the home cook?

The more you cook and grill, the better you will be at adjusting the level of salt and pepper to suit your palate. Because taste is subjective, I have opted in almost every recipe to list salt, pepper, and olive oil (what I call the Grilling Trilogy) without specific amounts. The reason is that the size of food is variable, as everyone who grocery shops knows—every chicken breast, steak, piece of fruit or vegetable, etc., is slightly different in shape and size. The most important thing to focus on is to make sure that all the surfaces of the food are lightly coated—lightly being the operative word—with olive oil and that a light (again, light is very important) sprinkle of kosher or sea salt is evenly distributed over the entire piece of food on both sides.

For seasoning novices, I recommend measuring out one-quarter teaspoon of salt, putting it in the palm of your hand, and sprinkling it over the food one pinch at a time. You can always add more salt, but it is impossible to fix food that is oversalted. As you salt the food, hold your hand as high over the food as possible when you are distributing the seasoning. The salt will be more evenly distributed and you'll reduce the possibility of having it all land on one section of the food. This sprinkling technique can be applied to pepper or any dry spice rubs as well as salt.

Once you follow these basic seasoning guidelines a few times, and taste your food, you'll know whether or not you need a lighter or heavier hand with the salt and pepper, and you'll become adept at seasoning to taste.

Here are a few things to remember:

- Many ingredients are naturally salty. If a recipe, sauce, or marinade calls for capers, anchovies, mayonnaise, salty cheese, soy sauce, etc., the recipe will get its saltiness from those ingredients and will need less or, sometimes, no added salt.
- Taste at every stage of the recipe (except when raw, for poultry, meat, and fish). The only way you will learn to season properly is to taste, taste, and taste—at every step—before you can adjust the salt, pepper, and other spices. Don't take a written recipe as the final word (except for baking); use it as your guideline to make the dish, adjusting flavoring as your palate deems necessary.
- It's better to undersalt slightly and serve prepared food with fleur de sel or a nice, coarse sea salt at the table. This allows people to finish seasoning their food tailored to their individual palates.

Big, Bold Flavor Enhancers

Crowd-pleasing barbecue is truly a work of art, combining sweet, sour, spicy, and smoky flavors. You can add flavor with marinades, rubs, mops, homemade barbecue sauces, fresh herbs, salsas, and wood chips.

Marinades

Marinades are a great way to flavor meat, including ribs. Marinades at their simplest have one acidic ingredient and usually a base ingredient of vegetable or olive oil. Good acidic choices include cider vinegar, lemon juice, pineapple juice, wine, beer, orange juice, and lime juice. Common flavoring elements include grated or minced fresh ginger, garlic, onion, hot sauce, ketchup, soy sauce, spices, Worcestershire sauce, and Asian chili sauce. Be careful when adding sugars because they burn quickly; it's similar to putting barbecue sauce on before grilling. By the time the meat is cooked, the outside will be burned.

Brines

Brining has become very popular in recent years, especially for lean cuts of meat like pork loin, chops, and country-style ribs, as well as chicken and turkey. In the brining process, the meat absorbs a portion of the seasoned salt and sugar solution, making the meat juicier and more flavorful. A brine technically only has to be a strong salt solution, but the sugar balances the salt and promotes browning. I call for kosher salt in my brines, but you can substitute table or sea salt—just use half as much. A simple brine formula is one cup of kosher salt and one-half cup of sugar to one gallon of water. (See also Basic Brine, page 35.)

While other meats may brine for a long time, because the bone to meat ratio is so small, soak ribs for 15 to 30 minutes, no more.

MARINATING KNOW-HOW

Marinades penetrate the meat with flavor. One note of caution when using acid-rich marinades: Soaking meat for too long can result in a mushy or overtenderized texture. Be careful not to put too much acid or other tenderizing ingredients in your marinade. For example, both ginger and pineapple contain natural enzymes that quickly break down or tenderize food. A little is great, but a lot of acidic ingredients or marinating for a long time will ruin your meat. Since marinades are acidic, always marinate in a glass, plastic, or stainless steel container, never in aluminum, which will react with the acid. This is what recipe instructions are referring to when they call for a "nonreactive bowl or container." The Instant Marinater works perfectly as a nonreactive vessel. I also like to use large, resealable plastic bags. The bags are airtight, and you can move the food through the plastic so all parts are exposed to the liquid easily and without any mess.

Spice and Barbecue Rubs

A spice or barbecue rub is a mixture of spices that is sprinkled or lightly "rubbed"—thus the derivation of the term—onto the ribs prior to cooking. Think of a rub as a dry marinade. Rubs add flavor and can help form a crispy crust on the ribs. The best way to use a rub is to put it on the meat about 20 minutes before you plan to cook it. This helps the spices to penetrate and season the meat.

Some people like to "rub" the ribs and other food that is going to be barbecued the night before. If you do this, make sure the rub mixture doesn't have any salt in it or it will dehydrate the ribs. "Rub" your food the right way by holding your hand at least a foot above the food and sprinkling back and forth over the food. The height and the back and forth motion help the rub to be evenly distributed. Then gently pat the rub into the food.

Never rub hard into the food, or you will damage the fibers and texture of the food and run the risk of overseasoning it.

Many varieties of premixed rubs are available commercially, but they are also easy to make at home. Common ingredients include salt (sea salt or kosher salt is best), white or brown sugar, black, red, and white peppers, paprika (sweet and smoky), granulated garlic and onion powders, dry mustard, cumin, fennel, parsley, thyme, and oregano. This list is by no means exhaustive. Let your culinary inner child go free and mix and match to your palate's delight.

Mops

A mop is a thin basting sauce that is "mopped" or brushed on the ribs (or other barbecue) during cooking. It can be a leftover marinade, although most barbecuers like to mix a special mop for the cooking process. Typical mops are mostly beer, water, apple cider, or some other neutral-flavored liquid. To this base, add whatever spices and seasoning you like, but be careful with the salt, as it is very easy to oversalt. To use a mop, check on the ribs periodically as they cook, about every 20 minutes. Baste the ribs with the mopping sauce and close the lid. If using wood chips, let the ribs cook unchecked for at least 30 minutes before adding the first mop.

Barbecue Sauces

For many people, barbecue sauce is the heart and soul of the barbecue flavor. The most popular types of barbecue sauces are sweet, red, tomato-based sauces, although there are some other varieties available. Vinegar sauces have made North Carolina famous, and yellow mustard-based sauces are popular in some parts of South Carolina and Georgia. There is even a mayonnaise-based sauce from Alabama. But typical sauces start with a base of either ketchup, American chili sauce, tomatoes, or tomato sauce and are heavily flavored with onions, garlic, and other aromatic vegetables like bell peppers or celery that have been cooked down and pureed into the liquid. The key ingredient is actually Worcestershire, as the tangy tamarind flavor in that sauce is what most of us associate with barbecue sauce. Other common ingredients include hot pepper sauce, cider vinegar, red wine vinegar, whiskey, honey, molasses or brown sugar, coffee, soy sauce, dried fruits, juices, herbs, and spices.

Remember, don't apply your barbecue sauce until the last 15 minutes of cooking time. This way, your food will be done inside and the sauce will coat it with a nice warm glaze. If you put the sauce on earlier, it may burn.

NOTE: Quick-cooking foods, such as boneless skinless chicken breasts, which take less than 20 minutes to cook, should be sauced during the final 5 minutes of the grilling time.

Select Recipes from Taming the Flame

Elizabeth Karmel

The Original Beer-Can Chicken
Tequila Sunrise Chicken
Chipotle Chicken Thighs
Buffalo-Style Chicken Wings
Chinese Five-Spice Chicken Salad with
    Purple Grapes
Salt-Cured Duck Breast with Fig Jam
Classic Backyard Burgers
Steakhouse-Style Cookout with à la Carte Sauces
Flat-Iron Steak with Pernod Butter and Grilled
    Frites
Beer-Soaked Filet Mignon Stuffed with Gorgonzola
Guinness-Marinated Flank Steak Sandwich
    with Grilled Onions and Boursin
Cumin-Rubbed Flank Steak with Chimichurri Sauce
Jack and Coke–Soaked Pork Chops
Crusty Double-Cut Pork Chops with Grilled Oranges
Smoky Pork Tenderloin Tacos
Honey-Marinated Sesame Pork Kabobs
Spicy Pork Roast with Pickled Peaches
Sheboygan Brat Fry
Lamb Chopsickles
Patio Daddy-O Shish Kabobs
Red Wine–Marinated Leg of Lamb with
    Roasted Cipollini Onions
Grilled Fish with a Ginger-Soy-Citrus
    Marinade
Salmon BLTs with Herbed Mayonnaise
Nantucket Swordfish with Browned Butter and
    Sautéed Pecans
Whole Fish with Thai Flavors
Firecracker Shrimp with Hot Pepper
    Jelly Glaze
Shrimp Margaritas with Avocados and
    Garden Tomatoes
Bacon-Wrapped Sea Scallops
Cape Porpoise Lobster Roll
Asparagus with Lemon-Truffle Vinaigrette
Portobello Burgers
Chinese New Year Pineapple Rings
Renaissance Ribs
Memphis in May World Championship Ribs
Chinese Take-Out Baby Back Ribs
Basic Brine
Pineapple–Lemon Juice Marinade
Hot-Hot-Hot Sauce Marinade

CHICKEN

The Original Beer-Can Chicken

I first discovered this method for cooking chicken—literally grilling a chicken set over a beer can—at the Memphis in May Barbecue competition in the early 1990s. I was so amazed that I couldn't stop talking about it. I'm not taking credit for the beer-can chicken craze, but I taught it to many distinguished culinary writers and chefs. It's a technique that is easy to love, and now more and more people are roasting a chicken perched on top of a beer can.

Makes 4 servings

Grilling Method: Indirect/Medium Heat
Special Equipment: Vacu Vin Instant Marinater

1	whole roasting chicken, 4 to 5 pounds, preferably Amish or organic
	Olive oil
3	tablespoons dry spice rub, divided, or Classic Barbecue Rub (page 33)
1	12-ounce can domestic beer, such as Budweiser

1. Remove the neck and giblets, and rinse the chicken inside and out if desired; pat it dry with paper towels. Coat the chicken lightly with oil and season with 2 tablespoons of the dry rub. Set aside.
2. Build a charcoal fire or preheat a gas grill. Open the beer can, pour out about ¼ cup of the beer, and make an extra hole in the top of the can with a church-key can opener. Sprinkle the remaining tablespoon of the dry rub inside the beer can. Place the beer can in the center of the cooking grate over indirect medium heat and sit the chicken on top of the beer can. The chicken will appear to be sitting on the grate.
3. Cover and cook the chicken for 1 to 1½ hours or until the internal temperature registers 165°F (74°C) in the breast area and 180°F (82°C) in the thigh. Remove it carefully to a platter, holding the can with tongs. Let it rest for 10 minutes before carving.

NOTE: When removing the chicken from the grate, be careful not to spill the contents of the beer can, as it will be very hot.
TIP: Follow the advice of chefs and brine your chicken before grill-roasting it beer-can style—use the Instant Marinater to brine the chicken (see page 1 for instructions).

Tequila Sunrise Chicken

I never soak my food in anything I would not drink. Well, there is nothing like a tequila sunrise to make you smile, giggle, or fall down laughing—and this tequila sunrise marinade makes chicken sing with flavor, which is my way of saying that this is a very happy, snappy recipe. Make an extra pitcher of sunrises for yourself—just be careful to make sure only the chicken gets sauced!

Makes 4 to 6 servings

Grilling Method: Indirect/Medium Heat
Special Equipment: Vacu Vin Instant Marinater

2	whole chickens, 3 to 4 pounds each
3	bunches green onions, trimmed
1½	cups fresh orange juice
1	cup tequila
½	cup grenadine
1	small white onion, roughly chopped
8	cloves garlic, roughly chopped
1	teaspoon kosher salt
	Freshly ground pepper
	Olive oil
	Lime wedges

1. Use a large knife or poultry shears to split each chicken down the middle into 2 halves. Pat the chickens dry with paper towels. Place the chickens and green onions in the Instant Marinater, a large bowl, or 2 large resealable plastic bags.
2. Whisk together the orange juice, tequila, grenadine, onion, garlic, salt, and pepper to taste in a medium bowl. Pour the marinade over the chickens and onions and turn several times to coat. Cover and refrigerate 30 minutes if using the Instant Marinater or

at least 4 hours if using a bowl or plastic bags.

3. Build a charcoal fire or preheat a gas grill. Remove the chickens and green onions from the marinade and discard it. Lightly brush the chickens and green onions with oil and season with salt. Place them on the cooking grate, skin-side up over indirect medium heat. Cover and grill for 30 to 45 minutes or until the chickens register 180°F (82°C) in the thickest part of the thighs and the juices run clear. Remove the chickens from the grill and let them rest for 10 minutes.

4. While the chickens rest, grill the green onions over direct medium heat for 6 to 8 minutes, turning occasionally until browned in spots and wilted.

5. Serve the chicken hot, garnished with grilled green onions and lime wedges.

TIP: You can also use a rib rack or roast holder to hold the half chickens upright during grilling.

Chipotle Chicken Thighs

Two years ago, I had the opportunity to travel the Isthmus region of Oaxaca, Mexico, with Suzanna Trilling, Mexican cooking expert and host of the television cooking show Seasons of My Heart. *The highlight of the trip was attending a* vela *or festival (called* Vela de la Virgen de la Candelaria*) where the women (including yours truly) dressed in hand-embroidered velvet costumes with lots of gold jewelry. The price of admission was a case of Coronitas (pony-size Corona beers—so small you finish them off before they have a chance to get warm) per person. To go with the beer, the local ladies also offered bowl after bowl of homemade food. A spicy and piquant chipotle chicken dish was made by many of the women, each adding her own special touch to the basic recipe. Be sure to serve this chicken with a wedge of lime and an ice-cold Corona.*

Makes 4 servings

Grilling Method: Indirect/Medium Heat
Special Equipment: Vacu Vin Instant Marinater

- 1   white onion, chopped
- 1   bunch fresh cilantro, chopped
- 1   7-ounce can chipotles in adobo
- 2   limes, 1 juiced and 1 quartered
     Kosher salt
- 2 to 3 cups mayonnaise
- 8   chicken thighs or 2 chickens, cut into pieces

1. In a blender, mix the onion, cilantro, chipotles with adobo sauce, and lime juice. Add a pinch of salt. Remove to the Instant Marinater or a large nonreactive bowl. Fold in 2 cups of mayonnaise. Taste and adjust the seasonings. If it is too hot, add more mayonnaise. Add the chicken pieces and refrigerate for 2 to 4 hours, turning occasionally, or 30 minutes in the Instant Marinater.

2. When ready to cook, build a charcoal fire or preheat a gas grill. Place the chicken, bone-side down, in the center of the cooking grate over indirect medium heat.

3. Cover and grill-roast until the breast meat near the bone registers 170°F (77°C) and the thigh meat registers 180°F (82°C), about 45 minutes. You do not need to turn the chicken pieces. If you don't have a thermometer, cook until the chicken is no longer pink and the juices run clear. Remove the chicken from the grill using tongs and a spatula to preserve the crust on the top of the thighs. Let the chicken sit for 10 minutes before serving.

Buffalo-Style Chicken Wings

This is the easiest chicken wing recipe you're bound to encounter, especially since the wings don't need to be marinated. All the flavor and the traditional sweet heat are added to the wings once they've crisped up on the grill. In memory of my favorite Buffalo, NY, native, Harold Herman, I call for serving them with Buffalo's favorite sides—blue cheese dip and celery sticks—but they are equally good on their own.

Makes 6 to 10 servings

Grilling Method: Combo/Medium Heat

> 4 to 5 pounds chicken wings or drummettes
>   (24 pieces)
>   Olive oil
>   Kosher salt
>   Freshly ground pepper
> 1 6-ounce bottle Louisiana hot sauce
> 2 tablespoons butter
> 1 tablespoon honey
>   Blue Cheese Lovers' Blue Cheese Dip
>   (recipe follows)
> 6 celery stalks, cut into sticks

1. Build a charcoal fire or preheat a gas grill. Pat the chicken pieces dry with paper towels. Coat them all over with olive oil and season with salt and pepper. Place the wings in the center of the cooking grate over indirect medium heat, cover, and grill for 20 to 25 minutes, turning once halfway through the cooking time.

2. Meanwhile, combine the hot sauce, butter, and honey in a small, heavy-bottomed saucepan. Bring to a gentle boil, whisking occasionally, and reduce the heat to low. Season to taste with salt and pepper. Divide the sauce, taking about $1/3$ to the grill to brush on the wings, keeping the rest warm. Turn the wings over and grill for the final 10 minutes and remove them from the grill.

3. Switch to direct medium heat. Pour the remaining sauce over the wings and toss to coat them evenly. Take the coated wings back to the grill and place them on the cooking grate. Cover and grill 4 to 5 minutes on each side or until very brown and caramelized. Remove from the grill onto a clean platter.

4. Serve hot, with the blue cheese dip and celery stalks on the side.

Blue Cheese Lovers' Blue Cheese Dip

I was tired of wimpy blue cheese dips, so I was thrilled when my friend John Mose shared his mother's recipe with me. It is pungent without being too strong, and the addition of garlic and shallots deepens the flavor of the blue cheese. I add a little more of the cheese and seasonings than the recipe calls for since I am at the top of the stinky cheese lover's scale. For best results use Societe Roquefort or another pungent blue cheese. Try the dip on a salad, veggies, chicken wings, or just about anything that needs a "dip" that rocks!

Makes 2 cups

> 1   cup mayonnaise
> $1/2$ cup sour cream
> 4   ounces quality blue cheese or more to
>   taste, crumbled
> $1^{1/2}$ tablespoons grated shallot or onion
> 1   tablespoon fresh lemon juice
> 2   cloves garlic, grated
>   Fine-grain sea salt
>   Freshly ground pepper

Combine all the ingredients except the salt and pepper in a large bowl, and refrigerate for at least 3 hours to let the flavors develop. Taste and adjust salt and pepper as needed. Serve chilled.

Chinese Five-Spice Chicken Salad with Purple Grapes

If you're tired of deli chicken salad but still love the ease of pulling a meal together out of what's in the fridge, try this refined version of the American standard. You can buy Chinese five-spice powder at most grocery stores; a shake or two of it will transport ho-hum into humdinger! The sweet-savory spice combination of the five spices (cinnamon, clove, fennel, star anise, and Szechuan peppercorns) complements the smoky grilled chicken and enhances the cool tang of the grapes. Serve the salad in a small lettuce leaf with Garlic Melba Toast, and you'll be the hit of your book or cooking club. This salad is even better after sitting in the fridge for a day, making it a great choice for a do-ahead party or picnic.

Makes 4 to 6 servings

4   boneless skinless chicken breast halves
    Olive oil
    Kosher salt
    Freshly ground pepper
$^1/_2$ cup mayonnaise, or more to taste
1   scant tablespoon Chinese five-spice
        powder
1   cup halved purple or red grapes
2   sticks celery, minced
1   head Boston or butter lettuce
$^1/_4$ cup toasted slivered almonds
16 to 24 pieces Garlic Melba Toast (recipe
        follows) or store-bought melba toast

1. Build a charcoal fire or preheat a gas grill.
    Rinse the chicken and pat it dry with paper
    towels. Brush with olive oil and
    season with salt and pepper. Place the
    chicken in the center of the cooking grate
    over direct medium heat, cover, and grill for
    about 15 minutes or until the meat is no
    longer pink and the juices run clear. Turn
    the chicken only once during cooking time.
2. Let the chicken cool. Meanwhile, mix the
    mayonnaise and five-spice powder in a
    large bowl.
3. Chop the cooled chicken into $^1/_2$-inch cubes
    and add them to the bowl with the dressing.
    Mix well, adding more mayonnaise if neces-
    sary. Add the grapes and celery and mix
    again. Add salt and pepper to taste and
    adjust the seasonings. Refrigerate for at least
    4 hours or preferably overnight to let the
    flavors develop.
4. When ready to serve, place a scoop of salad
    on the inside of a lettuce leaf and sprinkle
    with the almonds. Serve with Garlic Melba
    Toast.

Garlic Melba Toast

Makes 20 pieces

4   cloves garlic, grated
$^1/_2$ cup olive oil
1   loaf French bread, cut into $^1/_4$-inch slices

Preheat the oven to 250°F (121°C). Mix
the garlic and olive oil in a small bowl.
Place the bread rounds on a cookie
sheet and brush the tops with the garlic
oil. Bake for 1 to 2 hours or until completely crisp and golden. Serve warm or
let cool, then store in an airtight container for up to 2 weeks.

DUCK
Salt-Cured Duck Breast with Fig Jam

*One recent fall I was in the heart of Provence in
Arles, France, with my mother. We shopped the
weekly market until all the vendors had packed up
and then, famished, went looking for a place to have
lunch. We stumbled on a charming local restaurant
with gorgeous tablecloths and no tourists. La Mule
Blanche was a family affair where the wife sat in
front of the restaurant with a cash box and the hus-
band tended the bar. I almost never order duck in
restaurants, preferring to grill it myself, but I figured
that since I was in France, it would probably be okay.
Well, it was scrumptious and memorable. This recipe
is my recreation of that wonderful lunch. I added the
fig jam because the sweetness perfectly complements
the rich flavors of salt and rendered duck fat.*

Makes 4 servings

Grilling Method: Indirect/Medium Heat
Special Equipment: Vacu Vin Instant Marinater

4   skin-on boneless duck breasts
2   cups very coarse sea salt (not kosher)
1   cup packed dark brown sugar
1   tablespoon coarsely ground pepper
$^1/_4$ cup best-quality fig jam, preferably with
        whole figs or large pieces of fig
$^1/_2$ lemon, juiced (about 4 teaspoons)

1. Pat the duck dry with paper towels. Score
    the skin by making about 5 diagonal cuts
    across each breast, taking care not to cut
    completely through the skin. For fancier
    scoring, repeat the cuts in the opposite

direction, so that it creates a diamond pattern. Put the breasts in the Instant Marinater or a square, 8-inch disposable aluminum container. It should be deep enough to hold all 4 breasts with space in-between. Set aside. Mix the salt, brown sugar, and pepper and pour it over the duck. Cover and refrigerate for 4 hours or overnight.

2. When ready to cook, build a charcoal fire or preheat a gas grill. Remove the duck breasts from the pan and shake off the excess salt. Place the duck fat-side up in the center of the cooking grate over indirect medium heat, cover, and grill-roast for about 40 minutes. Turn duck over on the skin side and continue grilling until the skin is crispy and the meat is tender, 5 to 10 more minutes. (If the skin is not crisp, move duck to an area of direct heat, skin-side down, for 3 to 4 minutes to caramelize the skin.) When the skin is caramelized, return to an area of indirect heat and turn over to glaze.

3. When the duck is almost done, mix the jam with the lemon juice and brush it generously onto the skin of the duck breasts. Grill for 5 more minutes or until the fig glaze is set. Remove from the grill and let the breasts rest for 5 minutes before serving.

TIP: Contrary to popular duck cookery methods, I cook the duck breasts slowly, until they are cooked through, because I find them to be more tender and flavorful this way. If you like duck breasts served rare, alter the timing accordingly.

BEEF
Classic Backyard Burgers

I am one of those basic burger gals. Although I like changing my toppings as my mood dictates, I mostly crave a traditional flavor profile that I remember from my childhood. When I was a teenager, my best friends—known collectively as the Luasions—ate as many meals as we could at our neighborhood grill. Most days, we ordered these simple hamburgers. All they did was shape the patty, add a little salt and pepper, and fry them in butter, which gave the burgers the most divine crust! It is still the best hamburger that I have ever eaten. It hinges on two things: the best-quality ground chuck and mixing the meat only until it is combined. Overmixing the meat toughens the fibers.

Makes 6 servings

Grilling Method: Direct/Medium Heat

2   pounds ground chuck
    Kosher salt
    Freshly ground pepper
4   tablespoons ($\frac{1}{2}$ stick) unsalted butter, softened
6   slices cheddar or Swiss cheese
6   sesame seed buns
6   slices Vidalia or other sweet onion, optional
6   crisp lettuce leaves, optional
6   slices ripe tomato, optional

1. Build a charcoal fire or preheat a gas grill.
2. Being careful not to overwork the meat, season it with salt and pepper and mix just until combined. Gently shape the meat into 6 burgers of equal size and thickness (about $\frac{3}{4}$ inch thick). Make an imprint in the center of each patty with your thumb. Spread the top of each patty with a thin layer of soft butter.
3. Place the unbuttered side on the cooking grate over direct medium heat, cover, and grill for 4 minutes. Turn and spread the cooked side with a thin layer of butter. Continue grilling until the meat is no longer pink, 4 to 6 more minutes. If making cheeseburgers, top each burger with a slice of cheese after you turn it.
4. Meanwhile, butter both sides of the buns and grill them over direct medium heat until lightly toasted, 1 to 2 minutes.

5. Serve on the buttered rolls with a lettuce leaf, a slice of raw onion, and a slice of tomato. Serve with traditional condiments on the side.

Steakhouse-Style Cookout with à la Carte Sauces

I love hosting dinner parties because everyone always has more fun at someone's home than at a restaurant. This recipe celebrates the restaurant renaissance of steaks being served tableside with luxurious sauces. Try this build-your-own steak buffet by offering at least two of the options at your next party, and I promise you will be the talk of the town! The sauces can be prepared in advance and brought to room temperature just before serving.

Makes 4 servings

Grilling Method: Indirect/Medium Heat

4 New York strip steaks, about 1½ inches thick and ¾ pound each
   Olive oil
1 teaspoon kosher salt
1 teaspoon whole black peppercorns, coarsely ground

1. Build a charcoal fire or preheat a gas grill. Pat the meat dry with paper towels and allow it to come to room temperature about 20 to 30 minutes before grilling.
2. Just before grilling, brush both sides of the steaks with oil. Mix the salt and pepper together, and season the meat on both sides with the mixture.
3. Place the steaks on the cooking grate over indirect medium heat, cover, and grill for about 5 minutes. Turn the steaks and continue cooking for 7 to 10 more minutes for medium-rare. Remove the steaks from the grill and place them on a clean platter. Allow the steaks to rest at least 5 minutes but no longer than 10 minutes before serving them with a variety of sauces.

Mixed Herb Butter
Makes ½ cup

½ cup (1 stick) unsalted butter, softened
2 teaspoons minced fresh parsley
2 teaspoons granulated garlic
2 teaspoons mixed dried herbs, such as tarragon, basil, rosemary, thyme
   Fine-grain sea salt
   Freshly ground pepper

1. Combine the butter, parsley, garlic, and dried herbs in a small bowl. Mix together, mashing with the back of a fork to make sure all the ingredients are incorporated. Season to taste with salt and pepper, and mix well.
2. Meanwhile, cut a piece of plastic wrap about 6 inches long and spread it out flat. Spoon the soft butter mixture onto the plastic wrap and wrap it around the butter. Roll to make into a smooth log. Twist the ends to close them and refrigerate it at least 2 hours and up to 2 weeks, until ready to serve.

Blue Cheese Vinaigrette
This recipe is equally good served as a salad dressing or a steak sauce.

Makes 1 cup

⅓ cup white wine vinegar
1 teaspoon heavy whipping cream, at room temperature
⅔ cup olive oil or canola oil
¼ cup crumbled blue cheese
   Fine-grain sea salt
   Freshly ground pepper, optional

1. Whisk the vinegar and cream in a medium bowl. Slowly add the oil a little at a time, whisking until well incorporated (emulsified). Continue until all the oil is used.
2. Stir in the blue cheese and mix well. Season to taste with salt and pepper, if

desired. This can be made up to 2 days in advance and stored in a glass jar in the refrigerator. Shake before serving.

Anchovy-Caper Sauce

This can be used as a sauce or marinade for steaks. Don't marinate for too long because it is a salty mixture. The anchovies and capers should provide enough salt; but if you want to add more, season to taste with a fine-grain sea salt.

Makes 1 cup

6 anchovy fillets, drained and finely minced
4 cloves garlic, finely minced
1 tablespoon capers, drained and coarsely chopped
$^2/_3$ cup extra-virgin olive oil
Fine-grain sea salt, to taste (optional)

Combine the anchovies, garlic, and capers in a small bowl or a food processor. Slowly whisk in the olive oil or add it with the machine running. This can be made up to 2 days in advance and stored in a glass jar in the refrigerator. Shake before serving.

Flat-Iron Steak with Pernod Butter and Grilled Frites

My brother-in-law Karl is a steak frites aficionado. Together we've conducted serious (albeit pleasurable) research to find a cut of beef that is most similar to the steak used in France for this very simple and satisfying entrée. I recently discovered a new cut called the flat iron. The flat iron is a thin and flat steak (thus part of the name) that has a rich succulent flavor. It was introduced to the market under this name a few years ago, but it was previously sold as a petit steak or a top blade steak. I love grilling it because it cooks fast. With the addition of a compound butter spiked with Pernod, a little Dijon mustard, parsley, and some frites, it's like having a Paris bistro in your own backyard.

Makes 4 servings
Grilling Method: Direct/Medium-High Heat

Pernod Butter
$^1/_2$ cup (1 stick) unsalted butter, softened
1 small shallot, minced
3 sprigs fresh tarragon, chopped, or $^1/_2$ teaspoon dried tarragon
2 teaspoons Pernod or Ricard (pastis)
Fine-grain sea salt
White pepper

4 flat-iron steaks or other favorite steaks, about 1 inch thick and $^3/_4$ pound each
Olive oil
Kosher salt
Freshly ground pepper, optional
Chopped fresh parsley

1. Make the Pernod butter: Put the butter, shallot, and tarragon in a small bowl. Mix together, mashing with the back of a fork to make sure all the ingredients are incorporated. Add the Pernod and mix again. When the texture is smooth, season to taste with salt and pepper and set aside.
2. Meanwhile, cut a piece of plastic wrap about 6 inches long and spread it out flat. Spoon the soft butter mixture onto the plastic wrap and wrap it around the butter. Roll to make into a smooth log. Twist the ends to close them and refrigerate it for at least 2 hours and up to 2 weeks, until ready to serve.
3. Pat the steaks dry with paper towels.
4. Lightly brush both sides of the steaks with olive oil and season with the salt and pepper, pressing the spices lightly into the meat. Allow to stand at room temperature for 10 minutes before grilling.
5. Build a charcoal fire or preheat a gas grill.
6. Place the steaks on the cooking grate over direct medium-high heat for 8 to 10 minutes or until medium-rare, turning once halfway through grilling time. Use an instant-read thermometer to make sure the meat is done to your liking.

7. Remove the steaks from the grill and place them on a clean platter. Allow them to rest for 5 minutes. Cut the cold Pernod butter into 4 generous slices. Serve the steaks warm with the butter on top and grilled frites on the side. For a restaurant touch, garnish with chopped parsley, if desired.

Grilled Frites with Dijon Mustard

Makes 4 servings

Grilling Method: Direct/Medium-Low Heat

3 large baking potatoes, scrubbed
　Olive oil
　Fine-grain sea salt
　Freshly ground pepper
　Strong Dijon mustard, such as Amora or Maille

1. Build a charcoal fire or preheat a gas grill.
2. Leaving the skins on, cut the potatoes to resemble thick-cut french fries (about ½ inch thick). Soak them in a large bowl of ice water for 15 minutes. Drain the potatoes and pat them dry with paper towels. Put them in a resealable plastic bag and drizzle with just enough oil to coat all surfaces of the potatoes. Seal the bag and massage the contents to ensure even coating. Transfer the potatoes from the bag to a large bowl and sprinkle with salt and pepper.
3. Place the fries across the cooking grates so they won't fall through. Cover and grill over direct medium-low heat for 12 to 16 minutes, turning occasionally to mark both sides. When done, you should have grill marks on all sides of the potatoes, and they should be tender on the inside. If the potatoes are marked before they are tender, move them to the warming rack or another place of indirect heat to finish cooking without

burning. Serve immediately with strong Dijon mustard as a dipping sauce.

Beer-Soaked Filet Mignon Stuffed with Gorgonzola

Every May for the past 13 years, my buddy Lynne Wilkinson and I have barbecued together at the famous Memphis in May World Championship Barbecue Contest, aka the Mardi Gras of the Barbecue World. Whenever we are together we can't stop eating, drinking, laughing, and sometimes even dancing. But before the barbecue, we start the weekend off with her Memphis-style beer-soaked ("when you go to the fridge to get a beer, get one for the steaks as well; open your beer, take a sip, open another can and pour it on the steaks"), Gorgonzola-stuffed, bacon-wrapped filets. Talk about gilding the lily! But hey, we only live once, and it is mighty tasty.

Makes 4 servings

Grilling Method: Direct/Medium Heat
Special Equipment: Vacu Vin Instant Marinater

4 filet mignons, about 2 inches thick and ½ pound each
1 12-ounce bottle domestic beer of your choice
8 small chunks of Gorgonzola cheese, about 8 teaspoons
4 slices bacon
　Solid wooden toothpicks, soaked in water for 30 minutes
　Olive oil
　Kosher salt
　Freshly ground pepper

1. Put the filets in the bottom of the Instant Marinater or an airtight container and pour the beer over them. Place in the refrigerator. Marinate for 1 hour, turning once, or 20 minutes in the Instant Marinater.
2. Build a charcoal fire or preheat a gas grill. Remove the filets from the beer. Insert a grapefruit spoon or paring knife in the side of each filet to make an incision halfway into the filet. With a spoon, stuff 2 chunks

of the Gorgonzola into each incision. Wrap a piece of bacon around the side of each filet, covering the edges and the holes that the cheese went into. Secure the ends of the bacon with a wet toothpick. Brush the filets lightly with olive oil and season with salt and, if desired, pepper.

3. Place the filets on the grill over direct medium heat, cover, and cook for 9 to 12 minutes, turning occasionally to mark all sides and make the bacon crisp. The filets will be medium-rare and the cheese will be melted inside. Use an instant-read thermometer to make sure the meat is cooked as you like.

4. Remove the meat from the grill and place it on a clean platter. Let the filets rest for 5 minutes before serving.

Guinness-Marinated Flank Steak Sandwich with Grilled Onions and Boursin

During a trip to the Ballymaloe Cookery School in County Cork, Ireland—and more than a few hours logged in the local pub—I developed a definite fondness for Guinness. When I returned to the States, I started cooking everything from gingerbread to flank steak with the sudsy brown nectar. This recipe makes a great sandwich for any sports occasion. I usually serve it warm, but it is also perfect packed in a picnic and eaten at room temperature.

Makes 4 servings

Grilling Method: Direct/Medium Heat
Special Equipment: Vacu Vin Instant Marinater

2 pounds flank steak or top round steak, sometimes called London broil, at least 1 inch thick
1 14.9-ounce bottle Guinness beer
2 large red onions, cut into 1/2-inch slices
8 bamboo skewers, soaked in water for 30 minutes
Olive oil
Kosher salt

Freshly ground pepper
1 5.2-ounce container Boursin cheese, frozen
8 slices thick sourdough or country bread, optional

1. Pat the steak dry with paper towels. Put it in the Instant Marinater or a nonreactive container with a tight seal. Pour the Guinness over the steak and set aside.

2. Peel the onions and cut them into slices 1/2 to 3/4 inch thick. Put the onion slices on top of the steak. Cover the container and marinate in the refrigerator for 1 to 2 hours or 30 minutes in the Instant Marinater.

3. Build a charcoal fire or preheat a gas grill. When ready to grill, remove the meat and onions from the marinade and pat them dry. Thread the center of each onion slice with a bamboo skewer (they will resemble onion lollipops). Brush the steak and onions with a thin coating of oil and season with salt and pepper.

4. Place the steak and onions on the cooking grate over direct medium heat, cover, and sear. Cook for 6 to 8 minutes, then turn the steak and onions with a pair of tongs and sear the second side. Continue grilling another 6 to 8 minutes. Use an instant-read thermometer to determine if the meat is done to your liking. The steak and onions will take about the same amount of time to grill.

5. Remove the steak and onions from the grill and place them on a clean platter to rest for 5 minutes. While the meat is resting, shave a thin layer of Boursin on the top of the meat and the tops of the onions. (The steak and onions can be served at this point as a main course instead of as a sandwich.)

6. If serving as sandwiches, spread 1 side of the bread slices with olive oil and grill 1 to 2 minutes or until toasty and marked. Remove the bread from the grill and spread the untoasted sides with Boursin cheese.

7. Put 2 onion slices each on 4 pieces of bread and set aside. Slice the steak in long thin slices about ¼ inch thick. Place the slices of meat on top of the onions and top each with another piece of bread. Push down to compact the sandwiches a little before cutting them in half. Serve while still warm or wrap and refrigerate until ready to eat.

TIP: To get just the right amount of cheese, freeze the Boursin for at least 1 hour to make it easier to shave onto the top of the meat and onion.

Cumin-Rubbed Flank Steak with Chimichurri Sauce

This simple cumin, garlic, and smoked paprika rub and the chimichurri sauce elevate the humble flank steak into a signature dish. Chimichurri sauce originates from South America and tastes like a garlic-rich parsley pesto. This recipe can be served on small slices of baguette for a substantial cocktail party appetizer, on hearty whole-grain bread for a Dagwood sandwich, or sliced and drizzled with the chimichurri sauce and served with roasted new potatoes for a main course.

Makes 8 to 10 appetizer or 4 main course servings

Grilling Method: Direct/Medium Heat

Cumin Rub
1	teaspoon granulated garlic
½	teaspoon smoked paprika
½	teaspoon cumin seeds

1	flank steak, about ¾ inch thick and 1½ to 2 pounds each
	Olive oil
	Kosher salt

Chimichurri Sauce
2	cups loosely packed chopped fresh curly parsley, about one bunch
¾	cup olive oil

3 to 5	cloves garlic
3	tablespoons sherry wine vinegar or red wine vinegar
3	tablespoons fresh lemon juice
2	tablespoons minced shallot or onion
1	teaspoon kosher salt
½	teaspoon freshly ground pepper
½	teaspoon red chile flakes
1	baguette, sliced thinly (about ½ inch wide) Fleur de sel

1. In a small bowl, mix the rub ingredients until well combined. Set aside.

2. Pat the steak dry with paper towels. Trim it of any surface fat. Brush it lightly with olive oil. Press the rub into both sides of the steak.

3. Build a charcoal fire or preheat a gas grill.

4. Meanwhile, make the chimichurri sauce: Put all the ingredients in a blender or food processor and pulse until well chopped but not pureed.

5. Just before grilling, season the steak with salt. Place the meat on the cooking grate over direct medium heat, cover, and sear. Cook for 4 to 6 minutes. Turn the steak with a pair of tongs and sear the second side. Continue grilling 3 to 5 more minutes for medium-rare. Use an instant-read thermometer to test the meat.

6. Remove the steak from the grill and put it on a clean platter to rest for 5 to 10 minutes before carving. While the meat rests, spread the baguette slices with chimichurri sauce and set aside.

7. Cut the steak across the grain into thin diagonal slices. Place a slice on each piece of bread spread with the chimichurri sauce and sprinkle with a pinch of fleur de sel. Serve hot or warm.

NOTE: Chimichurri also makes a great marinade for fish, shellfish, and chicken, and a savory condiment for eating with everything grilled, as well as sandwiches, omelettes, and pasta.

PORK

Have you ever noticed that your pork chops almost always taste better in a restaurant than when you make them at home? The chef's secret is brining all lean cuts of pork before grilling or roasting. Try this in your Instant Marinater using the Basic Brine recipe on page 35 for all of these pork recipes. Brine up to 3 hours and eliminate the salt from the recipe, as the brine will supply the seasoning.

Jack and Coke–Soaked Pork Chops

Usually I drink my bourbon neat and eat my pork pulled, but in this recipe, I make an exception and put my sippin' whiskey where my pork is! You can't believe how delicious this unlikely marinade is. The sweet Coke syrup and the vanilla notes of the spirits are a perfect match. They deepen the flavor of the pork without making it too sweet. Since it's a sin to waste good whiskey, I boil and reduce the marinade (instead of discarding it) while the pork grills and use it to glaze the finished chops. Choose double-cut chops that take a little longer to cook or a boneless pork loin for best results.

Makes 4 servings

Grilling Method: Indirect/Medium Heat
Special Equipment: Vacu Vin Instant Marinater

4	double-cut pork chops, about 2 inches thick and 1 pound each
1	12-ounce can Coke or other cola
½	cup Tennessee whiskey, preferably Jack Daniel's, or bourbon
	Olive oil
	Kosher salt
	Freshly ground pepper

1. Pat the chops dry with paper towels. Set aside.
2. Pour the Coke and whiskey into the Instant Marinater or a container with a lid. Stir to mix. Put the pork chops in the marinade and turn each chop over to wet all surfaces with the marinade. Marinate for 30 minutes in the marinater or 1 hour in the refrigerator.
3. When ready to grill, build a charcoal fire or preheat a gas grill. Meanwhile, remove the chops from the marinade, drain to remove excess, then brush them lightly with olive oil. Season with salt and, if desired, pepper. Set aside.
4. Put the reserved marinade in a small saucepan and bring to a boil over high heat. Lower the heat and simmer for about 5 minutes, or until the marinade is reduced by about half.
5. Place the chops on the cooking grate over indirect medium heat, cover, and grill for 10 to 15 minutes. Turn the chops over and brush with the reduced marinade glaze. Continue grilling for about 15 more minutes, or until an instant-read thermometer placed in the thickest part of the chop registers 160°F (71°C).
6. Transfer the chops to a clean platter and let the meat rest for 5 minutes before serving. Serve extra glaze on the side if desired.

NOTE: I use the indirect method for this recipe because the marinade is very sweet. When using any sweet marinade or sauce, grilling by the indirect method will reduce flare-ups and prevent the pork from burning on the outside before the inside is cooked through.

Crusty Double-Cut Pork Chops with Grilled Oranges

These double-cut pork chops are coated with a sweet and salty rub and then cooked slowly over indirect heat until the outsides of the chops are deeply caramelized and crusty. That sounds good enough for me, but the real taste trick is in grilling cut oranges flesh-side down directly over the heat, then squirting the hot smoky orange juice on the pork chops just before serving.

Makes 4 servings

Grilling Method: Indirect/Medium Heat

Chop Rub

- ½ **cup packed dark brown sugar**
- 1 **tablespoon kosher salt**
- 1 **tablespoon sugar**
- ½ **tablespoon smoked or sweet paprika**
- ½ **tablespoon coarsely ground pepper**

- 4 **double-cut pork chops, about 2 inches thick and 1 pound each**
  Olive oil
- 2 **juice oranges, cut in half**

1. Make the chop rub: Mix all the ingredients together in a small bowl and stir until well combined. Store in an airtight container until ready to use.
2. Build a charcoal fire or preheat a gas grill. Pat the chops dry with paper towels. Brush lightly all over with oil. Set aside on a clean platter or tray. Using your hands or a spice bottle, sprinkle the meat all over with the chop rub. Pat gently into the meat to form a crust, but do not rub hard.
3. Put the chops back on the platter and let them sit for 5 minutes. When ready to grill, place the chops in the center of the cooking grate over indirect medium heat and cover. Grill for 15 minutes before turning. Turn and cook 10 to 15 more minutes, or until an instant-read thermometer registers 160°F (71°C). The outside of each chop should be crusty and the inside juicy and just a little pink.
4. Transfer the chops to a clean platter and let them rest for 5 to 10 minutes.
5. While the pork chops rest, put the orange halves on the cooking grate cut-side down, over direct medium-high heat (increase the heat if need be) for 5 minutes, or until the flesh is marked and the oranges are warmed through.
6. Remove the oranges from the grill and squeeze the juice from half of an orange

over each chop. Or, for a more dramatic presentation, serve a chop and an orange half together and let every- one squeeze their own juice over their meat. Serve hot.

Smoky Pork Tenderloin Tacos

This recipe delivers Mexican barbecue flavor in record time. The smoky three-chile rub flavors the meat, which is quickly seared over direct heat before grilling over a gentler indirect heat. The key to this recipe is to dry the meat of all its surface moisture and rub the dry meat with the spice rub. Add oil and salt just before grilling and let the meat rest for five minutes before serving with cilantro, salsa, and avocados.

Makes 4 to 6 servings

Grilling Method: Combo/Medium Heat

Smoky Three-Chile Rub (recipe follows)
- 2 **pork tenderloins, about 1 pound each**
  Kosher salt
- 8 to 12 **fresh corn tortillas**
- 2 **ripe avocados, pitted and thinly sliced**
- 1 **cup favorite salsa**
- 8 **sprigs fresh cilantro, finely chopped**

1. Build a charcoal fire or preheat a gas grill. Pat the tenderloins dry with paper towels. Put the meat into the bowl, rolling it in the Smoky Three-Chile Rub mixture, and patting the rub onto the meat, so it is evenly coated. Cover the meat with waxed paper or plastic wrap and let sit at room temperature for 10 minutes.
2. Season the meat with salt. Place the meat on the cooking grate over direct medium heat. Sear the meat on both sides, 2 to 3 minutes per side, until it is marked on all sides.
3. After searing, move the tenderloins to indirect medium heat. Cover and cook for 12 to 15 more minutes, or until an instant-read thermometer registers 160°F (71°C).
4. Transfer the meat to a carving board and let it rest for 5 to 10 minutes.

5. Warm the tortillas: Loosely wrap them in damp paper towels and microwave on high for 30 to 45 seconds or place them on the grill over indirect heat.
6. Slice the tenderloins into very thin pieces and serve hot with the warm tortillas, avocados, salsa, and cilantro in separate bowls so all guests can make their own tacos.

Smoky Three-Chile Rub

1 tablespoon New Mexican (or any other) chile powder
1 tablespoon chipotle chile powder or 1 additional tablespoon New Mexican chile powder
1 tablespoon sugar
$^1\!/_2$ tablespoon smoked paprika
$^1\!/_2$ tablespoon white pepper
1 teaspoon freshly ground pepper

In a medium bowl, combine the chile powders, sugar, paprika, and peppers.

Honey-Marinated Sesame Pork Kabobs

This simple honey, water, and rice wine vinegar marinade will make pork lovers everywhere swoon with delight. The marinade sweetens the pork chunks and enables the sesame seeds to stick, forming a crust that will get toasty and crunchy. This recipe makes a great appetizer or main course. For best results, cut kabob pieces from the tenderloin or a loin roast and marinate the chunks.

Makes 4 servings

Grilling Method: Indirect/Medium Heat
Special Equipment: Vacu Vin Instant Marinater

2 pork tenderloins, about 1 pound each
  Kosher salt
1 cup honey
$^1\!/_2$ cup water
$^1\!/_2$ cup unsweetened rice wine vinegar
$^1\!/_4$ cup toasted sesame oil
2 teaspoons Thai chili-garlic sauce (*sriracha*)

12 bamboo skewers, soaked in water for 30 minutes
$^1\!/_4$ cup sesame seeds
  Gingered Honey Sauce (recipe follows)

1. Pat the tenderloins dry with paper towels. Cut them into 1-inch chunks and season lightly with salt. Set aside while making the marinade.
2. Whisk together the honey, water, vinegar, sesame oil, and chili sauce. Put it in the Instant Marinater or a container with a lid. Add the pork and mix lightly to make sure that all the meat is exposed to the liquid. Put on the lid and refrigerate for 20 minutes in the Instant Marinater or 1 hour in the refrigerator.
3. Just before grilling, build a charcoal fire or preheat a gas grill. Remove the pork from the marinade and discard it. Thread the pork chunks onto skewers, using two skewers for each kabob.
4. Lay the sesame seeds flat on a piece of waxed paper and press both sides of the kabobs onto the seeds to coat the meat.
5. Place the kabobs on the cooking grate over indirect medium heat so the seeds do not burn before the meat cooks. Cover and grill for 8 to 10 minutes, turning once halfway through the grilling time, until the meat is firm to the touch.
6. Transfer the kabobs to a platter and let them rest for 5 minutes. Serve hot with Gingered Honey Sauce.

Gingered Honey Sauce

Makes 1/2 cup

1 cup apricot nectar
$^1\!/_2$ cup honey
1 knob fresh ginger (2 to 3 inches), peeled and grated
1 teaspoon dry jerk seasoning
1 teaspoon cornstarch mixed with 1 tablespoon water, optional (see Tip)

Pour the apricot nectar and honey into a small saucepan. Add the ginger and whisk to mix well. Bring to a boil and simmer until it is reduced by about one-third. Add the jerk seasoning and taste. Adjust the seasonings. Remove from the heat and let cool. Serve warm or at room temperature. If making in advance, refrigerate until using, then reheat slightly.

TIP: For a thicker sauce, add the cornstarch paste and bring the sauce to a boil over medium-high heat. Continue cooking, stirring, until the sauce thickens.

Spicy Pork Roast with Pickled Peaches

This is a recipe that you have to plan, but it's special and worth the effort. The peaches are pickled in a spicy sweet and hot liquid and set aside to rest for a day in the refrigerator. The peaches are drained, and the spiced peach juice becomes the marinade for the roast. When the roast is resting, you can gently sear the peach halves before serving them or serve them cold as a contrast to the hot roasted pork. Either way, it is a study in perfect porcine pleasure!

Makes 8 servings

Grilling Method: Indirect/Medium Heat
Special Equipment: Vacu Vin Instant Marinater

Pickled Peaches
    1   cup sugar
  1/2   cup white vinegar
  1/2   cup water
    1   tablespoon chopped crystallized ginger
   10   whole cloves
    1   cinnamon stick
    8   firm, ripe peaches, peeled, cut in half, and pitted

    1   pork loin roast, about 3 pounds
        Pickled peach liquid
        Olive oil
        Kosher salt
        Freshly ground pepper

1. Make the pickled peaches: Combine all the ingredients, except the peaches, in a large saucepan over medium heat and bring to a boil. Reduce to a simmer and add the peach halves. Bring back to a low boil, then reduce the heat slightly. Cook the peaches for 10 minutes, stirring occasionally to make sure all the peaches are submerged in the liquid. Remove from the heat and refrigerate for at least 1 day.
2. Transfer the peaches with a slotted spoon to a clean container and reserve the juice for the pork marinade.
3. Build a charcoal fire or preheat a gas grill.
4. Pat the pork dry with paper towels. Put the pork in the Instant Marinater or a container with a lid and add the reserved peach liquid. Marinate in the refrigerator for 30 minutes. After marinating, discard the marinade. Shake any excess liquid off the roast, brush it with olive oil, and season with salt.
5. Place the pork on the cooking grate over indirect medium heat, cover, and grill-roast for about 60 minutes or until an instant-read thermometer registers 160°F (71°C).
6. Transfer the roast to a carving board. Season with pepper, if desired, and let the meat rest for 10 minutes. Carve on the diagonal into thin slices and serve with the peaches.

Sheboygan Brat Fry

The first time I visited Sheboygan, WI, I asked every-one I saw where I could get a good brat (pronounced "braht"). The locals all looked at me like I was from a different world—which I clearly was, especially when I kept telling them that I wanted a grilled bratwurst not a fried one! For some reason, the traditional bratwurst cookouts are called "frys," even though there is no hot oil deep frying involved. As I was soon to learn, the best brats in Sheboygan are not at restaurants but made by natives for community fund-raisers and Green Bay Packer football games. Even though I prefer grilling then simmering the brats in beer, this recipe is the classic (simmering then grilling) way they do it in Sheboygan, the brat capital of the world.

Makes 4 main course or 8 appetizer servings

Grilling Method: Direct/Medium-Low Heat
Special Equipment: 5- to 8-quart stockpot

8	uncooked pork bratwursts
1	large white or yellow onion, divided
4 to 6	cans beer, such as Old Milwaukee
4	tablespoons (½ stick) unsalted butter
2	cloves garlic, chopped or smashed
	Pinch red chile flakes
8	hoagie or French rolls (hot dog buns are too small)
1	cup sauerkraut, warmed, preferably jarred not canned
	Brown mustard
	Prepared horseradish

1. Place the brats in the bottom of the stockpot. Cut the onion in half. Cut ½ into half-moon slices, chop the other half (for topping the cooked brats), and set aside. Add the half-moon slices of onions to the brats; add the beer, butter, and garlic. Make sure the brats are completely submerged in the beer; this will determine how much of the beer to use. Add a pinch of chile flakes. On the side burner of your grill or on the stove, bring the pot to a boil and then reduce the heat to a gentle simmer. Cook for 1 hour.

2. Meanwhile, build a charcoal fire or preheat a gas grill.

3. Remove the brats from the simmering liquid and put them on the cooking grate over direct medium-low heat, cover, and grill, turning occasionally until they are a deep brown all over. Return the brats to the stockpot and bring it back to a gentle boil. Immediately reduce the heat to very low and simmer for 20 minutes. The brats are now ready to serve directly from the stockpot. Do not let them sit out or they will get dry.

4. Spread mustard on 1 side of the buns and horseradish on the other. Place the brats in the buns. Cover with sauerkraut and sprinkle with the reserved chopped onions. Serve with good beer and German potato salad.

LAMB
Lamb Chopsickles

You may have enjoyed these finger-licking lamb chops at a wedding or a special event where guests gobble up the lamb chops with one hand while balancing a champagne flute with the other. Although I love the taste of these simple single-bone chopsickles, I much prefer eating them at a backyard cookout than a formal soirée. Because, just like ribs, I think that meat eaten right off the bone lends itself to a more down-home atmosphere. Serve the chops sizzling hot off the grill with a refreshing squeeze of lemon juice and plenty of napkins.

Makes 4 to 6 servings

Grilling Method: Direct/Medium Heat
Special Equipment: Vacu Vin Instant Marinater

⅔	cup extra-virgin olive oil
8	cloves garlic, minced or pureed
2	teaspoons capers, minced
2	lemons, zested and cut into wedges
16	single-bone lamb chops, cut from 2 frenched racks of lamb
	Kosher salt
	Freshly ground pepper
	Fleur de sel
	Lemon wedges

1. In a small bowl, mix the olive oil, garlic, capers, and zest and set aside.

2. Pat the chops dry with paper towels. Place the lamb chops in a single layer in the Instant Marinater or a shallow, nonreactive dish. Pour the olive oil mixture over the chops and turn the chops to make sure they are evenly coated. Cover and marinate in the refrigerator—turning the chops over once

halfway through—for 30 minutes in the marinater or 1 to 4 hours otherwise.

3. Just before grilling, build a charcoal fire or preheat a gas grill. Season the chops with salt and pepper. Place the chops on the cooking grate over direct medium heat, cover, and cook 3 to 4 minutes per side for medium-rare. Serve the chops literally hot off the grill. Before passing them to your guests, squeeze a lemon wedge over the chops and sprinkle with fleur de sel. Serve with lemon wedges.

TIP: Each lamb chop should have three- to four-inch-long "frenched" bones attached to the medallion of meat. Since these chops are to be served as finger food, the bones serve as the handle that your guests hold while eating.

Patio Daddy-O Shish Kabobs

In the fifties, shish kabobs were a favorite for entertaining around the barbecue. These popular skewers of meat and vegetables are said to be Turkish in origin, but many of us associate them with Greek cuisine. The classic shish kabob is still the preferred version of this famous food on a stick: peppers, tomatoes, white onions, button mushrooms, and chunks of lean meat. I love the flavor combination but find the tradition of threading all the foods together impractical since the ingredients take different amounts of time to cook. In my recipe, I assemble the skewers by the type of food so you can remove each from the grill when it is perfectly done.

Makes 6 servings

Grilling Method: Direct/Medium Heat
Special Equipment: Vacu Vin Instant Marinater

1   orange, zested and juiced
1   lemon, zested and juiced
¼   cup olive oil
3   cloves garlic, minced
1   tablespoon coarsely chopped fresh
      rosemary or 2 teaspoons dried
      rosemary

3   pounds boneless lamb (from leg or
      shoulder), cut into 2-inch chunks
28   bamboo skewers, soaked in water for
      30 minutes
1   large red onion, cut into 1½-inch wedges
2   yellow bell peppers, cut into 3-inch
      squares
8   ounces medium mushrooms, stems
      trimmed
6   ripe Roma tomatoes, cut in half
      Sea salt
      Freshly ground pepper

1. In a medium bowl, whisk together the juices, zests, olive oil, garlic, and rosemary. Arrange the lamb chunks in a single layer in the Instant Marinater or a glass dish and pour the marinade over it. Cover and refrigerate for 20 minutes in the marinater or 1 to 2 hours otherwise, shaking every now and again to coat the lamb evenly.

2. When ready to cook, build a charcoal fire or preheat a gas grill.

3. To assemble the kabobs, put the vegetables on a cutting board with the skewers nearby. Drain the meat from the marinade (discard marinade). Thread the meat onto 2 skewers, so they resemble a ladder. Leave room in between the meat so the pieces cook evenly. You should have about 4 kabobs.

4. Repeat the skewering process with the onion, peppers, mushrooms, and tomatoes, using 2 bamboo skewers for each kabob. Brush all the kabobs with oil and season with salt and pepper.

5. Place the kabobs in the center of the cooking grate over direct medium heat, turning to sear all sides. Cook to the desired degree of doneness, 8 to 10 minutes for the lamb to reach medium-rare. The meat and vegetables will take different amounts of time to cook. The tomatoes will be done first, the mushrooms next, and then the meat, onions, and peppers.

6. As the skewers are done, remove them from the grill. Place them on a clean platter. Let

the meat rest for 5 minutes while you unskewer the vegetables. Serve the shish kabobs surrounded by the grilled veggies.

Red Wine–Marinated Leg of Lamb with Roasted Cipollini Onions

I usually don't see much of a reason to marinate foods overnight, especially since too much acid in the marinade can ruin the texture of the meat, turning it into mush. But with a hearty bone-in leg of lamb, soaking it in a red wine marinade overnight per-fumes the meat and deepens the flavor. It also tints the meat a very pleasing light pink color. I marinate the cipollini onions with the lamb for the same rea-son. While the lamb cooks, reduce the marinade with a cup of balsamic vinegar until thickened to make a gravy that bursts with flavor!

Makes 6 servings

Grilling Method: Indirect/Medium Heat
Special Equipment: Vacu Vin Instant Marinater

1	bone-in leg of lamb, 6 to 7 pounds, excess fat trimmed
6	cloves garlic, minced or pureed Olive oil
2	tablespoons dried thyme
1	bottle red wine, such as Pinot Noir, Shiraz, or Beaujolais
1/2	cup whole-grain mustard
3	tablespoons coarsely cracked pepper, toasted
16	cipollini onions, unpeeled Kosher salt

1. Pat the lamb dry with paper towels. The day before you are going to grill the lamb, combine the garlic, 3 tablespoons of olive oil, and the thyme. Rub the lamb all over with this mixture. In the Instant Marinater or a large glass or nonreactive container, combine the wine, mustard, and pepper until all the ingredients are equally distrib-uted. Add the lamb and onions and

marinate, covered in the refrigerator overnight, turning occasionally to submerge all surfaces with the marinade.

2. About 20 minutes before you are ready to cook, build a charcoal fire or preheat a gas grill.

3. Remove the lamb and onions from the marinade (discard marinade) and pat them dry. Brush them with olive oil and season with salt. Place the lamb in the center of the cooking grate over indirect medium heat. Cover and grill for 1 1/2 to 2 hours, until an instant-read thermometer registers 140°F (60°C) (medium-rare) in the roast's thickest part. During the final 40 minutes of the lamb's cooking time, put the onions on the cooking grate or warming rack over indirect heat and roast them until soft and the sugars are oozing out of the skin, about 40 minutes.

4. Remove the lamb and onions from the grill, tent loosely with foil, and let rest for 15 minutes before carving and serving.

FISH
Grilled Fish with a Ginger-Soy-Citrus Marinade

This marinade is good on almost any fish and takes just a few seconds to whisk together. I created it one night when I was testing the Vacu Vin Instant Marinater. The marinater literally forced the flavor into the fish in only five minutes and the lemon zest tasted fresh, sparkling, and bright—as if I just zested it—even after grilling for 20 minutes. The marinater is one of the few pieces of special equipment that I recommend, but if you don't have one, you'll still get great flavor if you marinate the old-fashioned way—in a covered, nonreactive bowl in the fridge.

Makes 4 servings

Grilling Method: Indirect/Medium Heat
Special Equipment: Vacu Vin Instant Marinater

¼   cup olive oil
¼   cup toasted sesame oil
3 to 5 cloves garlic, grated, or more to taste
1   1-inch knob fresh ginger, grated, or more
       to taste
2   tablespoons rice vinegar (not sweetened)
2   tablespoons low-sodium soy sauce (such
       as Kikkoman)
1   tablespoon Thai chili-garlic sauce
       (*sriracha*)
1   lemon, zested and cut into wedges
       Kosher salt
4   fresh fish fillets, about 1¼ pounds total,
       such as wild salmon, mahi-mahi,
       pompano, shark

1. Combine the olive oil, sesame oil, garlic,
   ginger, rice vinegar, soy sauce, chili sauce,
   zest, and a pinch of salt. Mix well. Add the
   fish to the marinade, making sure all surfaces are coated. Cover and marinate for
   5 to 30 minutes in the Instant Marinater
   or in the refrigerator up to 1 hour in a
   nonreactive bowl. Turn occasionally to coat
   all sides.
2. Build a charcoal fire or preheat a gas grill.
3. Remove the fish from the marinade and
   gently shake off excess. Put the fish on the
   cooking grate, skin-side down, over indirect medium heat. Grill for about 15 to
   20 minutes without turning, or until done
   but pink in the center. Do not overcook.
4. Sliding the spatula between the bottom of
   the fish and the skin, remove the fish and
   place it on a platter. While the fish rests,
   increase the heat to high to crisp up the
   skin (it only takes about 2 minutes).
   Remove the skin from the grill and serve it
   with the moist fish. Garnish with lemon
   wedges, if desired.

TIP: Chili-garlic sauce, or *sriracha*, is that delicious pungent sauce in the clear bottle or jar
with a kelly-green plastic top and a picture of a
rooster. It is easily found in Asian grocery stores
or on the Internet.

TIP: There are two options that deliver the best
grated ginger and garlic for a marinade. One is
the Microplane kitchen tool and the other is the
SuperGrater ceramic grater. Both these tools rev-
olutionize all grating tasks, from cheese to ginger,
garlic, nutmeg, and chocolate. They are a must-
have for any home cook who likes to make short
work of grating. The SuperGrater is particularly
suited to garlic and ginger, and the Microplane
works best for hard cheese and nutmeg.

Salmon BLTs with Herbed Mayonnaise

*This sandwich is best served in the summer, when fresh
tomatoes abound and you are looking for a new way
to use them. The freshness of wild salmon pairs perfectly with the smoky bacon, acidic tomatoes, crunchy
lettuce, and cool herbed mayo. If you want to take
this sandwich one step further, leave the salmon skin
on the grill until it gets crisp and substitute it for the
bacon. I guarantee this will be one recipe you'll make
again and again. In a pinch, you can flavor
Hellmann's mayonnaise (my favorite brand) with the
garlic and herbs or, better yet, make the homemade
mayo in advance—it will keep refrigerated for a week
and is good for anything that calls for plain mayo.*

Makes 4 servings

Grilling Method: Indirect/Medium Heat

4   wild salmon fillets, about 6 ounces each,
       1 inch thick
       Olive oil
       Kosher salt
       Freshly ground pepper
8   slices bread from a rustic oval loaf, grilled
       on 1 side only
½   cup Herbed Mayonnaise (recipe follows)
12   slices (about 8 ounces) best-quality
       bacon, cooked and drained
2   tomatoes, cut in slices
4 to 8 crisp leaves romaine, cleaned and dried

1. Build a charcoal fire or preheat a gas grill.
2. Pat the salmon fillets dry with paper towels, brush them lightly with oil and season
   with salt and pepper.

3. Place the salmon, skin-side down, on the cooking grate over indirect medium heat, cover, and grill for 10 to 12 minutes. When the salmon begins to bubble at the skin, take a flat spatula and, turning it upside down, separate the flesh of the fish from the skin. Leave the skin to continue cooking. Remove from grill and transfer to a clean platter, letting it rest for a few minutes.

4. Spread the ungrilled side of each slice of bread with Herbed Mayonnaise. Place a piece of salmon on each slice of bread. Top with the bacon (or crispy salmon skin). Layer with the tomato and lettuce. Put the tops of the sandwiches in place. With a long, sharp knife, cut the sandwiches in half and serve immediately.

Herbed Mayonnaise

Makes 2 cups

1	large egg, at room temperature
1	large egg yolk, at room temperature
3	tablespoons fresh lemon juice, divided
2	tablespoons minced fresh chives, basil, and tarragon
1	tablespoon strong Dijon mustard
1/2	lemon zested
	Fine-grain sea salt
	Freshly ground pepper
1	cup olive oil
1/2	cup light olive oil or untoasted walnut oil

1. In a food processor fitted with a steel blade, combine the egg, egg yolk, and 1 tablespoon of the lemon juice. Pulse to mix.

2. Add the herbs, mustard, zest, a pinch of salt and pepper, and process until fairly smooth. With the motor running, slowly add the oils through the feed tube of the food processor. The mayonnaise will begin to thicken; watch closely and add the oil until it is the right consistency.

3. Taste the mayonnaise and adjust the seasonings, adding more lemon juice (the mayonnaise should be tart), herbs, salt, and pepper to suit your taste. Transfer to a storage container with an airtight lid. Cover and refrigerate for at least 2 hours to develop the flavors before using. The mayonnaise can be prepared up to 3 days in advance and will keep for 1 week in the refrigerator.

Nantucket Swordfish with Browned Butter and Sautéed Pecans

In 1983, I packed up my duffel bag and headed off to Nantucket to work—and play—for the summer. Little did I know that it would be a great culinary experience as well. In addition to scalloping with a fifth-generation fisherman, I ate out at all the great restaurants—most now defunct. At every dinner, it seemed that at least half the table would order swordfish with béarnaise sauce. When I started grilling, I remembered that dish and decided that I liked the richness of the sauce but that it needed some crunch.

The browned butter is easy enough for anyone with patience to make, and the pecans sauté and lightly brown as the butter slowly turns color. It not only looks good on a plate, but the flavor combination is in perfect harmony. The sauce can be made in advance and gently reheated just before serving. This recipe would also be good with any firm white fish such as tilapia, halibut, or sturgeon.

Makes 4 servings

Grilling Method: Direct/Medium Heat

1/2	cup (1 stick) unsalted butter
1	cup pecan pieces
	Fine-grain sea salt
	White pepper
4	center-cut swordfish steaks, 10 to 12 ounces each, about 1 inch thick
	Olive oil

1. Build a charcoal fire or preheat a gas grill.
2. Put the butter in a cold sauté pan. On medium-low heat, slowly melt the butter. Add the pecans and let them brown and toast as the butter slowly browns. Season lightly with salt and white pepper. You will need to watch the pan closely as the butter can burn very quickly. When the butter reaches a dark caramel color, remove it from the heat, cover, and set aside. Either keep it warm or gently reheat before topping the fish.
3. Brush the fish steaks on both sides with oil. Season with salt and pepper. Place them on the cooking grate over direct medium heat, cover, and grill about 5 minutes on each side, until the fish is opaque and releases easily from the grill.
4. Place the fish on a clean platter. Let the fish rest for 3 to 5 minutes. Top with the brown butter and pecans. Serve immediately.

Whole Fish with Thai Flavors

A few years ago, my friend Bob Blumer convinced me to go with him on a bike tour of Thailand—from Chang Rai to Chang Mai. This wasn't a tour for wimps or those seeking white tablecloth restaurants! During the 10-day trip, we averaged 100 kilometers a day and at night we ate the most amazing food at backroad huts, where often we were the only people there—certainly the only foreigners. As often as we could, we would order fish grilled whole over a wood fire and seasoned with garlic and chilies. In the cool night air, the steaming fish and ice-cold Singha beer made 100 kilometers on a bike seem like a small price to pay for the meal.

Makes 4 to 6 servings

Grilling Method: Indirect/Medium Heat
Special Equipment: Vacu Vin Instant Marinater

1 or 2 cleaned whole fish, such as grouper, sea bass, snapper, or catfish, 3¹/₂ to 4 pounds total
Olive or peanut oil

1   **small knob fresh ginger (1 to 2 inches), grated**
3   **cloves garlic, grated**
2   **teaspoons Thai chili-garlic sauce (such as** *sriracha*)
1   **lime, juiced**
2   **teaspoons fish sauce**
1   **teaspoon toasted sesame oil**
2   **limes, sliced in rounds, divided**
    Solid wooden toothpicks, soaked in water for 30 minutes

1. Build a charcoal fire or preheat a gas grill.
2. Brush the fish all over with oil and set aside.
3. Meanwhile, make the marinade, which will resemble more of a paste than a traditional marinade. Mix the ginger, garlic, chili paste, lime juice, fish sauce, and sesame oil in a small bowl. Taste and adjust the seasonings as necessary. If it needs more salt, add a few more drops of fish sauce, which provides the salty notes in this recipe.
4. Spread the paste generously and evenly inside the fish and add half of the lime slices. Secure the fish with a wet toothpick threaded through the cut in the stomach. This will prevent the limes and seasonings from spilling out. Place in the Instant Marinater and then in the refrigerator for 5 to 10 minutes.
5. Place the fish on the cooking grate over indirect medium heat, cover, and grill 30 to 35 minutes of total cooking time.
6. When the fish is done and opaque in the thickest part, remove it from the grill. Let the fish rest for 3 to 5 minutes. Serve hot, with the remaining slices of lime.

SHELLFISH
Firecracker Shrimp with Hot Pepper Jelly Glaze

These shrimp explode with flavor. The marinade sings with pungent ginger and chile-rich notes tempered by the sweet rice wine called mirin. Do not substitute fresh for the dried ginger in the marinade because it will overly tenderize the delicate shrimp, resulting in a tough and chewy texture. These skewers are full of sweet heat and make an impressive presentation, especially when served stuck into a wedge of fresh watermelon. Bring it out and watch the fireworks go off in your guests' eyes.

Makes 4 to 6 servings

Grilling Method: Direct/Medium-Low Heat
Special Equipment: Vacu Vin Instant Marinater

24   jumbo shrimp, about 1½ pounds, peeled, tails on
12   bamboo skewers, soaked in water for 30 minutes
¼   cup mirin (sweetened rice wine)
2   tablespoons toasted sesame oil
1   tablespoon low-sodium soy sauce
2   teaspoons ground ginger
2½   teaspoons unsweetened rice vinegar
2   heaping tablespoons hot pepper jelly
2   teaspoons sesame seeds, toasted

1. Build a charcoal fire or preheat a gas grill. If frozen, thaw shrimp in cold running water just before cooking.
2. In a nonreactive bowl, combine mirin, sesame oil, soy sauce, ginger, and 2 teaspoons of the vinegar. Set aside.
3. Heat the hot pepper jelly and the remaining ½ teaspoon vinegar in a small saucepan until warm and liquid, stirring occasionally. Keep warm over a very low heat until ready to use.
4. Meanwhile, prepare the shrimp. Place the shrimp in the Instant Marinater or a resealable plastic bag and pour the mirin marinade over them. Place in the refrigerator for 20 minutes.
5. Make sure the grilling grate is very clean. Skewer the shrimp by inserting bamboo skewers on either side of shrimp so that the shrimp resemble the rungs of a ladder. You will end up with a total of 6 skewers with 4 shrimp on each skewer; make sure

there is room between each shrimp.

6. Make sure the grill is only at medium-low heat, or the sugar in the marinade will burn and blacken before the shrimp are cooked. If your grill is too hot, lower the burners of a gas grill and lift the lid of both gas and charcoal grills until the cooking grate has cooled off.
7. When the grill is the right temperature, place the skewers on the cooking grate over direct medium-low heat for 4 to 5 minutes. Turn the shrimp over (since the marinade contains sugar, you may need to use a spatula to pry the edges of the shrimp as you turn the skewers with tongs). Once all the skewers are turned, lightly coat the cooked side of the shrimp with the pepper jelly glaze using a long-handled basting brush. Cook for an additional 4 to 5 minutes or until the shrimp are cooked through.
8. Remove from the grill and sprinkle with the sesame seeds. Let rest for a few minutes. Serve hot.

TIP: Freeze extra soaked bamboo skewers in foil or a resealable plastic bag so they'll be ready at a moment's notice.

Shrimp Margaritas with Avocados and Garden Tomatoes

This recipe is one that I never get tired of making or eating and neither do my guests. The beauty of this dish is that it is loaded with flavor, impressive to serve, and has to be made in advance, making it a great choice for a low-maintenance dinner party. Mix the avocado and tomatoes just before serving to layer the flavors and keep all the ingredients fresh and chunky. For a festive appetizer, serve this in a margarita glass rimmed with a mixture of kosher salt, lime zest, and smoked paprika. Splurge and sprinkle with fleur de sel before serving.

Makes 4 to 6 servings

Grilling Method: Direct/Medium-High Heat
Special Equipment: Vacu Vin Instant Marinater

1 pound unshelled large shrimp
2 tablespoons olive oil
$^{1}/_{4}$ cup tequila, preferably 100 percent Blue
    Agave
$^{1}/_{4}$ cup fresh lime juice
$^{1}/_{4}$ cup fresh orange juice
2 tablespoons ketchup
2 tablespoons green Tabasco or other
    jalapeño hot sauce
1 bunch green onions, green tops only,
    finely chopped
    Kosher salt (omit if serving with fleur
    de sel)
    Freshly ground pepper
2 cups diced ripe heirloom or garden
    tomatoes, drained
2 large ripe avocados, diced
1 small white onion, chopped
    Lime wedges, optional
18 saltine crackers (or more)
    Fleur de sel or coarse sea salt, optional

1. Build a charcoal fire or preheat a gas grill.
2. If frozen, thaw shrimp in cold running water just before cooking. Place the shrimp in a nonreactive bowl. Mix them with olive oil until well coated.
3. Place the shrimp on the cooking grate over direct medium-high heat, cover, and grill until pink and almost cooked through, 4 to 6 minutes, turning them once halfway through the cooking time. Remove the shrimp from the grill and let them cool completely.
4. Meanwhile, whisk together the tequila, citrus juices, ketchup, and Tabasco in the Instant Marinater. Peel and cut the shrimp into large pieces (about $^{1}/_{2}$ inch) and toss them with the tequila mixture. Chill in the refrigerator for 15 minutes. Add the green onion tops and return to the refrigerator for 1 hour.
5. Just before serving, season the mixture with salt and pepper to taste. (Omit this

step if serving with fleur de sel.) Gently fold in the tomatoes and avocados, mixing well. Using a slotted spoon, portion into individual serving bowls or margarita glasses. Garnish with a sprinkling of white onion and a wedge of lime. If you haven't already salted the mixture, sprinkle each serving with fleur de sel. Serve immediately with saltine crackers.

Bacon-Wrapped Sea Scallops

When I was a guest chef at the James Beard Foundation House, I started the meal with these crispy bacon-wrapped scallops, and they were eaten in a flash! Since there are so few ingredients, it is essential to use the absolute best quality bacon and scallops. I recommend Niman Ranch or another specialty bacon and large Alaskan sea scallops. A bigger scallop is better since it won't overcook during the time it takes to cook the bacon.

Makes 8 to 10 servings

Grilling Method: Direct/Medium-Low Heat

1 pound sea scallops, preferably Alaskan
8 ounces center-cut bacon, such as
    Niman Ranch
    Solid wooden toothpicks, soaked in water
    for 30 minutes

1. Build a charcoal fire or preheat a gas grill.
2. Pat the scallops dry with paper towels. Cut the bacon in half width-wise and wrap $^{1}/_{2}$ piece around each scallop, securing with a wooden toothpick. Cover and let the bacon come to room temperature before grilling.
3. Place the scallops on the cooking grate over direct medium-low heat, cover, and grill until the bacon is crisp, about 5 minutes on each side. If you have trouble getting the bacon crispy by the time the scallops are done, you can precook the bacon in a microwave on high for 30 seconds before wrapping the scallops.

4. Remove from the grill, let rest a few minutes then serve immediately.

NOTE: Bacon is great on its own, but it is even better as a flavor enhancer. If you are ready to expand your bacon horizons, check out The Bacon of the Month Club and the artisanal bacons available from www.thegratefulpalate.com.

Cape Porpoise Lobster Roll

If you travel a little off the beaten track in Maine, you will find the Cape Porpoise Lobster Company in Cape Porpoise. Their main business is selling whole lobsters to restaurants or consumers via overnight mail. However, they also make the best lobster roll, bar none! Their secret is keeping the number of ingredients to a minimum—heavy on the lobster and a buttery grilled bun. One summer evening, I grilled a half dozen chicken lobsters and made this rendition, which is pretty close to the original! If you live near a lobstering town, purchase the rolls made especially for this sandwich.

Makes 4 servings

Grilling Method: Direct/Low Heat

- 4 grilled or boiled lobsters, claw and tail meat removed
- $\frac{1}{2}$ cup mayonnaise, preferably Hellmann's
- 1 lemon, cut into wedges
- $\frac{1}{2}$ cup (1 stick) unsalted butter, melted
- 4 lobster or hot dog rolls

1. Cut the lobster meat into large $1\frac{1}{2}$- to 2-inch chunks. Fold the meat into the mayonnaise and season with a squirt or two of lemon juice. Add 1 tablespoon of hot melted butter, mix to coat, and adjust the seasonings if necessary. Cover and refrigerate for 1 hour or up to 1 day.
2. If you have the grill on, just before serving, butter both the insides and outsides of the rolls. Grill the buttered surfaces until golden brown (like the top of a grilled cheese sandwich) over direct low heat. (Alternately, heat the buttered bread in an oven or toaster oven.)
3. Spoon the lobster mixture into the warm buns and serve immediately, with a wedge of lemon, if desired.

VEGETABLES

Asparagus with Lemon-Truffle Vinaigrette

I didn't think grilled asparagus could get any better until I created this "truffle lemonade" to dress up my favorite grilled veggie for a friend's birthday party. Try it, and use any leftover dressing on fresh salads or grilled fish. The little bit of cream in the recipe keeps the vinaigrette from separating and rounds out the sharp flavors of the lemon juice and the truffle oil.

Makes 4 servings

Grilling Method: Direct/Medium Heat

Lemon-Truffle Vinaigrette
- $\frac{1}{3}$ cup fresh lemon juice (about $2\frac{1}{2}$ lemons)
- 1 teaspoon heavy whipping cream, at room temperature
- $\frac{1}{3}$ cup olive oil or canola oil
- $\frac{1}{8}$ to $\frac{1}{4}$ cup truffle oil
  Sea salt
  Freshly ground pepper, optional

- 1 pound fresh asparagus (large stalks with firm deep green or purplish tips and moist ends)
  Olive oil
  Kosher salt, about 1 teaspoon

1. Build a charcoal fire or preheat a gas grill.
2. Make the vinaigrette: Whisk together the lemon juice and cream in a small bowl. Slowly add the olive oil a little at a time, whisking until well incorporated (emulsified). Continue, whisking in the truffle oil to taste. Season to taste with sea salt and pepper. Resist the urge to overseason since the grilled asparagus will be well seasoned. Set aside.

3. Rinse the asparagus and snap or cut off the bottom 1 inch of each spear. Place the asparagus in a resealable plastic bag and drizzle just enough oil in the bag to coat all the spears. Seal the bag and turn the spears to coat them evenly in the bag. Sprinkle with salt, reseal the bag, and turn it again to evenly distribute the salt. (This is the "plastic bag trick" and can be used for any food.)

4. Place the asparagus on the cooking grate over direct medium heat, cover, and grill for 5 to 7 minutes or until well marked and caramelized. Turn the spears during cooking to grill each side. The asparagus should begin to brown in spots (this indicates that the natural sugars are caramelizing) but should not char.

5. Remove the asparagus from the grill, drizzle with the vinaigrette, and serve immediately.

Portobello Burgers

Portobello mushrooms are nature's meat substitute and perfectly suited for hearty sandwiches or burgers. This colorful medley of grilled portobello, peppers, fresh basil, prosciutto, and parmesan cheese is dressed with roasted garlic mayonnaise. Equally good hot or cold, the vegetables can be grilled ahead and the sandwiches assembled when needed—perfect picnic fare for summer concerts in the park.

Makes 6 servings

Grilling Method: Direct/Medium Heat
Special Equipment: Vacu Vin Instant Marinater

2	red or yellow peppers, or both
1/2	cup balsamic vinegar
1/4	cup olive oil, plus more as needed
1	teaspoon dried rosemary
	Kosher salt
	Freshly ground pepper
6	large portobello mushrooms, the same size as the rolls
6	kaiser or onion rolls
1	head garlic, roasted

1/2	cup best-quality mayonnaise
1	bunch fresh basil, leaves only
8	ounces Parmigiano-Reggiano cheese, thinly sliced (slice with a vegetable peeler)
8	ounces thinly sliced prosciutto di Parma, optional

1. Build a charcoal fire or preheat a gas grill.

2. Place peppers on cooking grate and grill over direct medium heat until skin is charred. Remove peppers from grill with tongs and place in paper bag; let sit for 30 minutes. Take peppers out of bag; remove skin and seeds, and cut into strips.

3. Combine the balsamic vinegar, olive oil, rosemary, salt, and pepper. Add the peppers and let them marinate in the Instant Marinater or nonreactive bowl for up to 3 days in the refrigerator.

4. Clean the mushrooms with a damp paper towel, remove the stems, and set aside.

5. Just before grilling, remove the peppers from the marinade and add the mushrooms. Let them sit for 5 minutes. Drain the mushrooms from the marinade. Place the mushrooms on the cooking grate gill-side up over direct medium heat, cover, and grill for 8 to 10 minutes. Turn them over for and grill 1 minute more or until tender.

6. Split the kaiser rolls in half. Brush them lightly with oil. Place them, cut-side down, on the grill for 2 to 3 minutes or until lightly toasted. Meanwhile, mix the garlic and mayonnaise until smooth.

7. When the rolls are toasted, assemble the sandwiches by spreading the insides of the rolls with garlic mayonnaise and layering a mushroom, peppers, basil leaves, cheese (you may have some left over), and optional prosciutto on top. Season with salt and pepper, if desired. Place the top roll on each sandwich and cut in half before serving. Alternatively, you can plate the portobellos and other ingredients without bread for an elegant and delicious appetizer.

Chinese New Year Pineapple Rings

Pineapple is one of those fruits that can fit into either a sweet or savory recipe, depending on the marinade or seasonings. This recipe's savory Asian flavors set off fireworks when served with grilled meat or fish. Because the marinade is so versatile, it can be doubled and used to marinate chicken, pork, and other fish at the same time as the pineapple. If you want to turn the marinade into a serving sauce, bring it to a gentle boil for three minutes while the meat and fruit are grilling.

Makes 4 servings

Grilling Method: Indirect/Medium Heat
Special Equipment: Vacu Vin Pineapple Slicer and Instant Marinater

1	fresh pineapple, sliced in rings
2	green onions, finely chopped
$^1/_4$	cup toasted sesame oil
3	tablespoons low-sodium soy sauce
1	knob fresh ginger (1 to 2 inches), grated
3	limes, 2 juiced, 1 cut into wedges
1	tablespoon maple syrup or brown sugar
	Pinch Chinese five-spice powder

1. Put the pineapple slices in a nonreactive bowl or the bottom of the Instant Marinater. Mix the onions, sesame oil, soy sauce, ginger, lime juice, maple syrup, and five-spice powder in a small bowl to make the marinade.
2. Pour the marinade over the pineapple, tossing gently to make sure all the surfaces are coated with marinade. Cover and refrigerate for 20 minutes.
3. When ready to grill, build a charcoal fire or preheat a gas grill.
4. Shake the excess marinade off the pineapple rings but do not dry them. You want as much marinade as possible to cling to the fruit. Place the rings on the cooking grate over indirect medium heat, cover, and grill for about 6 minutes on each side. The pineapple should be tender, well-marked, and warmed through. Serve or use as directed in a recipe.

RIBS
Renaissance Ribs

I created these ribs quite by accident one year at Memphis in May. After barbecuing about 50 slabs of ribs for a party, I was tired of the traditional "barbecue" rub and tried a concoction of Italian herbs, red chile flakes, and sesame seeds. I had no idea what the result would be, but everyone loved them. So much so that I even featured them at a dinner that I did for the New York City–based culinary organization The James Beard Foundation. These ribs are so popular in my house that I usually make a few slabs with this rub every time I make ribs. Serve them "dry," with only a light coating of olive oil. The oil will bring out the flavor of the pork and spices; barbecue sauce will mute the flavors. For the same reason, I do not recommend using wood chips to smoke the meat as it cooks.

Makes 4 to 8 servings

Grilling Method: Indirect/Medium-Low Heat

Italian Spice Rub

2	tablespoons sesame seeds
2	tablespoons granulated garlic
1	tablespoon dried Mediterranean oregano
1	tablespoon red chile flakes
2	teaspoons dried rosemary
2	teaspoons dried lemon peel

4	racks baby back ribs, about 3 pounds each (optional)
$^1/_2$	cup fresh lemon juice (about 2 lemons)
2	cups water
	Kosher salt
	Olive oil (preferred) or favorite barbecue sauce (optional)

1. Make the spice rub: Combine the sesame seeds and spices in a small bowl until well mixed.
2. Build a charcoal fire or preheat a gas grill, setting up the grill for indirect heat.
3. Remove the silver skin from the back of the ribs, if desired. Combine the lemon juice and water and set aside. Place the ribs in a

plastic resealable bag or nonreactive container and cover them with the lemon juice mixture. Marinate for 20 to 30 minutes (no longer or the meat will get mushy).

4. Remove the ribs from the marinade and sprinkle them front and back with the spice rub. This can be done up to 1 day in advance, and they can be kept wrapped in aluminum foil in the refrigerator. Just before cooking, season with salt.

5. Place the ribs, bone-side down, in the center of the cooking grate or in a rib holder or rack over indirect medium-low heat. Grill covered (at about 325°F [163°C], if your grill has a thermometer) for 1½ to 2 hours or until the meat is tender and has pulled back from the ends of the rib bones.

6. Leave the ribs untended for the first 30 minutes—this means no peeking. If the ribs start to burn on the edges, stack them on top of one another in the very center of the grill and lower the heat slightly. Twenty minutes before serving, brush the ribs with a light coating of olive oil or the optional barbecue sauce.

7. Remove the ribs from the grill and let them rest 10 minutes before cutting into individual or 2 to 3 rib portions.

Memphis in May World Championship Ribs

Memphis-style ribs are as dry as Kansas City–style ribs are wet! I created these very simple ribs after nosing around the rigs of many of the championship teams. The secret to these ribs is the thin mop that you baste the ribs with during the final hour of cooking time.

Makes 4 to 8 servings

Grilling Method: Indirect/Medium-Low Heat
Special Equipment: Vacu Vin Instant Marinater

Memphis in May Mop
1   12-ounce beer, preferably Budweiser
½   cup favorite barbecue sauce
1   tablespoon Classic Barbecue Rub (recipe follows) or favorite barbecue rub

4   slabs back ribs, about 3 pounds each
     Hickory wood chips, soaked in water for 30 minutes (optional)
     Apple Cider Vinegar Marinade (recipe follows)
     Olive oil
     Classic Barbecue Rub (recipe follows)
     Favorite barbecue sauce, optional

1. Make the mop: Combine the ingredients in a bowl and mix well. Let them sit for 10 minutes, stirring occasionally to make sure all the carbonation is gone. Place the mop in a squeeze bottle or leave it in the bowl. Set aside until ready to use. The mop can be made in advance and refrigerated for up to 1 week.

2. Build a charcoal fire or preheat a gas grill. Set up the grill for indirect heat; if using wood chips, place the soaked chips directly on the charcoal or in the smoking box of a gas grill.

3. Remove the silver skin from the back of the ribs, if desired. Put the ribs in the Instant Marinater or a resealable plastic bag or nonreactive container with the Apple Cider Vinegar Marinade for 15 minutes (no longer or the meat will become mushy), turning frequently to make sure all the surfaces are wet and marinating.

4. Remove the ribs and let them sit for 5 minutes. Discard the marinade. Brush the ribs with a light coating of olive oil and sprinkle liberally with the spice rub. Let them sit, covered, for 15 to 20 minutes.

5. Place the ribs, bone-side down, in the center of the cooking grate or in a rib holder or rack over indirect medium-low heat. Grill covered (at about 325°F [163°C], if your grill has a thermometer) for 1½ to 2 hours or until the meat is tender and has pulled back from the ends of the rib bones.

6. Leave the ribs untended for the first 30 minutes—this means no peeking, especially important if using wood chips. After the first 30 minutes, baste the ribs with the mopping sauce every 20 minutes. If the

ribs start to burn on the edges, stack them on top of one another in the very center of the grill and lower the heat slightly. Ten minutes before the ribs are done, stop mopping them.

7. Remove the ribs from the grill and let them rest for 10 minutes before cutting into individual or 2 to 3 rib portions. Serve with warmed sauce on the side, if desired.

Apple Cider Vinegar Marinade

Makes 4 cups; enough for
4 racks of ribs

1   cup apple cider vinegar
3   cups water

Mix the vinegar and water. Use to marinate ribs or other cuts of pork and chicken. Soak meat no longer than 30 minutes.

Classic Barbecue Rub

This rub has all the classic barbecue notes: salt, spice, sweet, and smoke. It is particularly great on ribs, but it works with pork chops and tenderloin, chicken, and even catfish for a beautifully authentic low 'n' slow barbecued flavor.

Makes about 1 cup

2   tablespoons smoked paprika
2   tablespoons kosher salt
3   tablespoons sugar
2   tablespoons brown sugar
1   tablespoon ground cumin
1   tablespoon chili powder
1   tablespoon freshly ground pepper
$1/2$ tablespoon cayenne
1   tablespoon onion powder
1   tablespoon garlic powder
1   tablespoon celery salt
1   teaspoon oregano, crushed

Combine all the ingredients in a medium bowl and mix well. For a smoother rub, process the ingredients in a spice grinder until well combined and all pieces are

uniform (the rub will be very fine and tan in color). Use it to rub on meat before grilling. Extra rub can be stored in an airtight container for up to 6 months.

Chinese Take-Out Baby Back Ribs

These ribs remind me of early Sunday evenings waiting for take-out at my favorite Chinese restaurant. I usually snack on these ribs while I wait for the rest of the order to cook. The combination of the sweet and spicy marinade and sauce makes these Asian-flavored ribs explode with flavor. These ribs are truly yin and yang—with the sweet and spicy balancing each other—and rely on a fresh sprinkling of sea salt just before serving to bring out the sweetness of the ribs.

Makes 4 to 8 servings

Grilling Method: Indirect/Medium-Low Heat
Special Equipment: Vacu Vin Instant Marinater

Asian Marinade
1   cup sherry
$3/4$ cup low-sodium soy sauce
$1/2$ cup chopped green onions, about 1 bunch
$1/4$ cup red wine vinegar
$1/4$ cup sugar
$1/4$ cup toasted sesame oil
2   small knobs fresh ginger (1 to 2 inches long), peeled and grated, about 1 tablespoon
1   teaspoon granulated garlic
1   teaspoon red chile flakes
    Pinch freshly ground pepper

Hoisin-Style Barbecue Sauce
2   tablespoons peanut or olive oil
1   small onion, chopped
3   cloves garlic, chopped
1   cup plus 2 heaping tablespoons hoisin sauce, divided
$1/2$ cup low-sodium soy sauce
$1/2$ heaping cup red currant or seedless raspberry jelly
$1/3$ cup red wine vinegar

2 small knobs fresh ginger (1 to 2 inches
    long), peeled and grated, about
    1 tablespoon
1 tablespoon Thai chili-garlic sauce
    (*sriracha*), or more to taste
1 tablespoon brown sugar
1 tablespoon molasses
    Kosher salt
    Freshly ground pepper

4 slabs baby back ribs, about 3 pounds each
    Olive oil
    Kosher salt
    Freshly ground pepper
    Fleur de sel or other sea salt (optional)

1. Make the marinade: Combine the ingredients in a medium bowl. Set aside until ready to use. If making up to 24 hours in advance, add all ingredients except the onions and store, covered, in the refrigerator. Add the onions just before marinating.
2. Make the barbecue sauce: Heat the oil in a heavy saucepan over medium heat for about 2 minutes. Sauté the onion and garlic until translucent, about 10 minutes. Add 1 cup of the hoisin sauce, the soy sauce, jelly, vinegar, ginger, chili sauce, brown sugar, and molasses. Simmer for 30 minutes or until slightly thickened. Whisk in the 2 remaining tablespoons hoisin sauce. Season to taste with salt and pepper. Let the sauce cool and set it aside.
3. Meanwhile, build a charcoal fire or preheat a gas grill. Set up the grill for indirect heat.
4. Remove the silver skin from the back of the ribs, if desired. Place the ribs in the Instant Marinater, a resealable plastic bag, or a nonreactive container and cover them with the marinade. Soak for 20 minutes (no longer or the meat will get mushy), turning frequently to make sure all the surfaces are wet and marinating.
5. Remove the ribs from the marinade and let them sit for 5 minutes. Discard the marinade. Place the ribs, bone-side down, in the center of the cooking grate or in a rib holder or rack over indirect medium-low heat. Grill, covered (at about 325°F [163°C], if your grill has a thermometer), for 1½ to 2 hours or until the meat is tender and has pulled back from the ends of the rib bones.
6. Leave the ribs untended for the first 30 minutes (no peeking). If the ribs start to burn on the edges, stack them on top of one another in the center of the grill and lower the heat slightly. Twenty minutes before the ribs are done, unstack them if necessary and brush them with barbecue sauce. (Don't sauce the ribs too soon; the high sugar content of the hoisin sauce causes it to burn easily.)
7. Remove the ribs from the grill and let them rest for 10 minutes before cutting into individual or 2 to 3 rib portions. Just before serving, sprinkle the ribs with sea salt or fleur de sel. This step is essential as the fresh salt brings out the sweetness of the sauce. Serve with warmed sauce on the side, if desired.

TIP: Sriracha and hoisin sauce are available in the Asian section of a large grocery store or at any Asian market.

TIP: Grating the ginger maximizes the flavor for the marinade and sauce, meaning more ginger flavor for the ribs. To get 2 tablespoons for the recipes, you will need a knob of fresh ginger that is 4 to 5 inches long. Peel the ginger with a vegetable peeler and use either my GrillFriends SuperGrater or a Microplane grater. Alternatively, you could puree the ginger in a food processor, but you will need to be careful not to pulverize it.

TIP: For an extra-pretty presentation of these Asian-flavored ribs, cut the ribs into 2-bone portions and tie a fresh chive or the green part of a green onion around the rib. Make a double knot and cut the ends, leaving 1-inch pieces on the rib bundles. Sprinkle toasted sesame seeds on the ribs and serve stacked up on a square or other geometric platter.

BASIC BRINE AND SIMPLE MARINADES

Basic Brine

8	quarts water, divided
1	cup sugar or sweetener (honey, maple syrup, brown sugar)
1	cup kosher salt

1. Boil 2 quarts of the water, and add the sugar and salt, stirring until completely dissolved. Add the rest of the water (or ice to speed the process) and let it come to room temperature before submerging the meat or poultry. Add extra water if necessary to cover meat. (Do not put raw meat in a hot brine.)

2. Cover and refrigerate for up to 24 hours—the larger the piece of meat, the longer it might need to soak. Tenderloin or chops only need 30 to 60 minutes.

NOTE: Don't season brined meats with salt; the brining takes care of the seasoning. Pat dry, brush with oil, and grill—it's that simple!

Pineapple–Lemon Juice Marinade

Makes 4 cups

1	cup canned pineapple juice
1/2	cup fresh lemon juice (about 2 lemons)
2	cups water
1/2	cup vegetable oil

Mix the juices, water, and oil. Use to marinate ribs or other cuts of pork, chicken, or salmon. Marinate meat no longer than 30 minutes or it will start to break down.

Hot-Hot-Hot Sauce Marinade

This is a trick I picked up when I lived in New Orleans. On the weekends, I would travel to the swampy bayous and go to cookouts that featured this simple but stunning marinade. It took a lot of coercing and a few drinks to get this trick out of my host! If you use this marinade, skip the spice rub and use a sprinkling of kosher salt and a coating of olive oil. The trick: The meat is marinated in a straight solution of Louisiana hot sauce.

Makes enough for 4 racks of ribs or 3 pounds of chicken wings

2	6-ounce bottles Louisiana Brand hot sauce or Trappey's hot sauce (see Tip)

Use to marinate ribs or chicken wings. Soak meat no longer than 30 minutes. If you are nervous about the heat factor, dilute with 1/2 cup of water.

TIP: Louisiana Brand hot sauce (much milder than Tabasco) is distributed nationally, but if you can't find it, use 1 small bottle of Tabasco, 1/2 cup white vinegar, and 3 cups of water or more to taste.

TIP: To get the maximum flavor out of pepper (and other dried spices), toast whole peppercorns in a dry skillet over medium-high heat until you can barely see a wisp of smoke and smell the spice, 3 to 5 minutes. The toasting process releases the spice's volatile oils and maximizes the flavor—and efficacy—of the spice. Toast peppercorns or whole spices before grinding and you'll find your spice rubs will explode with flavor.

Be **Wine Smart**

Vacu Vin is an international manufacturer and distributor of innovative food- and wine-related products for home and professional use, which are characterized by their practical applications in daily circumstances. It all began in 1983, when Mr. Bernd Schneider, founder of Vacu Vin, came up with the idea for the Vacuum Wine Saver. His idea for the Wine Saver sprang directly from the taste of spoiled wine. Together with his brother John, an engineer, he developed a device to preserve open bottles of wine. Today the Vacuum Wine Saver is used in over 30 million households in more than 75 countries throughout the world.

Their love of wine inspired them to invent other wine products geared toward storing, cooling, and serving wine. This information has been prepared for you by Vacu Vin so you may enjoy wine with all of your grilled meals.

Pairing Food and Wine

The Vacu Vin Instant Marinater will help you make your meals tastier than ever. We also know that what you drink with your meals will affect the pleasure of your dining experience; and the quality and taste of the wines you drink, in particular, make a big difference.

Use this wine and food pairing chart. It will make you wine smart!

The table below shows you how to easily choose a wine from the right taste category to accompany your favorite foods.

Storing Wine

Once a wine is uncorked, its quality deteriorates due to exposure to oxygen (oxidation). How quickly this happens depends on the strength of the wine. Reseal an open bottle with the Vacu Vin Wine Saver to delay this process. For sparkling wines, use the Vacu Vin Champagne Saver.

A real cellar is, of course, the ideal location for keeping wine, but fortunately there are plenty of alternatives if you haven't got a cellar. Store wine in closets, under the stairwell or under the bed. To store your wine in a good visible location, the Vacu Vin Wine Rack Flexible is a good solution. This luxury wine rack is easy to assemble and flexible so that it can be configured into various shapes.

Vacu Vin Wine Saver: The reusable rubber cap and the vacuum pump keep wine at its best. A "click" sound tells you when you have reached the optimum vacuum level.

WINE Smart CHART

	WHITE WINES						RED WINES			
Cold Appetizers	6	5	4	3	2	1	1	2	3	A
Salads with fish										
Salads with meat							■			
Smoked fish										
Hot Appetizers	6	5	4	3	2	1	1	2	3	A
Vegetable quiche							■			
Warm salad with fish										
Snails										
Asparagus										
Pasta	6	5	4	3	2	1	1	2	3	A
Spaghetti à la bolognese							■			
Lasagne							■			
Pizza							■			
Fish and Shellfish	6	5	4	3	2	1	1	2	3	A
Steamed mussels										
Steamed fish with hollandaise sauce										
Fried fish							■			
Poultry	6	5	4	3	2	1	1	2	3	A
Roasted or grilled chicken							■			
Duck or pheasant								■	■	
Meat	6	5	4	3	2	1	1	2	3	A
Grilled pork							■	■		
Veal							■			
Barbecued beef								■		
Roasted or grilled lamb							■	■	■	
Cheese	6	5	4	3	2	1	1	2	3	A
Cream cheese							■			
Blue cheese										
Goat's cheese							■			
Desserts	6	5	4	3	2	1	1	2	3	A
Ice cream alone or with fruit	■									
Cookies and cakes or pies	■									
Nuts	■									■

How to read the Wine Smart Chart

6	very sweet
5	sweet
4	semi-sweet
3	mellow dry
2	dry
1	very dry
A	aperitifs (port, sherry)
1	light and drinkable
2	soft and fruity
3	full-bodied and robust

Cooling Wine

If a white wine is served cooler than 46°F (8°C), some of the flavor will disappear. Vacu Vin has brought several sophisticated coolers onto the market. Traditionally, the only means for cooling a wine were the ice bucket and the refrigerator. But the ice bucket requires effort, and the refrigerator is slow. Vacu Vin Rapid Ice® Coolers, available in many different bottle sizes, are like icy coats. They are chilled in the freezer, then slipped over a bottle of white wine to chill it in a few minutes to the right serving temperature. Red wine is often served too warm, given that today's "room temperature" is higher than it used to be. Just slip a Rapid Ice Cooler over the bottle, and the problem is solved. And there is the Vacu Vin Rapid Ice Champagne Cooler for the sturdier sparkling wine bottles.

Vacu Vin Rapid Ice Cooler

Serving Wine

A good wine glass is sufficiently large and tapers slightly toward the top, in order to hold as much of the wine's bouquet in the glass as possible (smelling wine is essential to tasting it). A standard portion of wine is about 4 fluid ounces (125 mL); thus, a large glass will not be more than one-half to two-thirds full. Using the Wine Server Crystal makes pouring easy and drip-free.

Wine Server Crystal

Index

A

Anchovy-Caper Sauce, 13
Appetizers, food and wine pairing with, 36
Apple Cider Vinegar Marinade, 33
Asian Marinade, 33
  for Pineapple Rings, Chinese New Year, 31
Asparagus with Lemon-Truffle Vinaigrette, 29–30
Avocados and Garden Tomatoes, Shrimp Margaritas with, 27–28

B

Baby Back Ribs, Chinese-Take-Out, 33–34
Bacon
  in Filet Mignon, Beer-Soaked, Stuffed with Gorgonzola, 14–15
  Salmon BLTs with Herbed Mayonnaise, 24–25
  Sea Scallops, -Wrapped, 28–29
Balsamic Marinade, for Portobello Burgers, 30
Barbecue Rub
  about, 4–5
  Classic, 33
Barbecue Sauce
  Hoisin-Style, 33–34
  ingredients for, 5
Beef
  Burgers, Classic Backyard, 11–12
  Filet Mignon, Beer-Soaked, Stuffed with Gorgonzola, 14–15
  Flank Steak, Cumin-Rubbed, with Chimichurri Sauce, 16
  Flank Steak Sandwich, Guinness-Marinated, with Grilled Onions and Boursin, 15–16
  Flat-Iron Steak with Pernod Butter and Grilled Frites, 13–14
  Steakhouse-Style Cookout with à la Carte Sauces, 12–13
  and wine pairing, 37
Beer
  in Brat Fry, Sheboygan, 20–21
  Chicken, Beer-Can, The Original, 7
  Filet Mignon, -Soaked, Stuffed with Gorgonzola, 14–15

Flank Steak Sandwich, Guinness-Marinated, with Grilled Onions and Boursin, 15–16
Beer-Can Chicken, The Original, 7
Bell Peppers, in Shish Kabobs, Patio Daddy-O, 22–23
BLTs, Salmon, with Herbed Mayonnaise, 24–25
Blue Cheese
  Dip, Blue Cheese Lovers', 9
  Vinaigrette, 12–13
Boursin, Flank Steak Sandwich, Guinness-Marinated, with Grilled Onions and, 15–16
Brat Fry, Sheboygan, 20–21
Brine
  Basic, 35
  formula for, 4
Buffalo-Style Chicken Wings, 8–9
Burgers
  Classic Backyard, 11–12
  Portobello, 30
Butter(s)
  Browned, and Sautéed Pecans, Nantucket Swordfish with, 25–26
  Herb, Mixed, 12
  Pernod, Flat-Iron Steak with Grilled Frites and, 13–14

C

Cape Porpoise Lobster Roll, 29
Caper-Anchovy Sauce, 13
Cheese. See also specific cheeses
  and wine pairing, 37
Chicken
  Beer-Can, The Original, 7
  boneless skinless breasts, saucing, 5
  Salad, Chinese Five-Spice, with Purple Grapes, 9–10
  Tequila Sunrise, 7–8
  Thighs, Chipotle, 8
  and wine pairing, 37
  Wings, Buffalo-Style, 8–9
Chile(s)
  Chipotle Chicken Thighs, 8
  Pepper Jelly Glaze, Hot, Firecracker Shrimp with, 26–27
  Smoky Three-, Rub, 19
Chimichurri Sauce, Cumin-Rubbed Flank Steak with, 16

Chinese Five-Spice Chicken Salad with Purple Grapes, 9–10
Chinese New Year Pineapple Rings, 31
Chinese-Take-Out Baby Back Ribs, 33–34
Chipotle Chicken Thighs, 8
Chop Rub, in Crusty Double-Cut Pork Chops with Grilled Oranges, 17–18
Cipollini Onions, Roasted, Red Wine-Marinated Leg of Lamb with, 23
Citrus-Ginger-Soy Marinade, Grilled Fish with a, 23–24
Coke and Jack-Soaked Pork Chops, 17
Combo grilling method, 2
Cumin-Rubbed Flank Steak with Chimichurri Sauce, 16

D

Desserts-wine pairing, 37
Dip, Blue Cheese, Blue Cheese Lovers', 9
Direct grilling method, 2
Dry rub. See Rub(s)
Duck
  Breast, Salt-Cured, with Fig Jam, 10–11
  and wine pairing, 37

F

Filet Mignon, Beer-Soaked, Stuffed with Gorgonzola, 14–15
Firecracker Shrimp with Hot Pepper Jelly Glaze, 26–27
Fish. See also Shellfish
  Anchovy-Caper Sauce, 13
  Grilled, with a Ginger-Soy-Citrus Marinade, 23–24
  Salmon BLTs with Herbed Mayonnaise, 24–25
  Swordfish, Nantucket, with Browned Butter and Sautéed Pecans, 25–26
  Whole, with Thai Flavors, 26
  and wine pairing, 37
Flank Steak
  Cumin-Rubbed, with Chimichurri Sauce, 16
  Sandwich, Guinness-Marinated, with Grilled Onions and Boursin, 15–16

Flat-Iron Steak with Pernod Butter
  and Grilled Frites, 13–14
Food and wine pairing, 36–37
Frites, Grilled, with Dijon Mustard,
  14

G

Garlic
  in Chimichurri Sauce, Cumin-
    Rubbed Flank Steak with, 16
  and Lemon Marinade, for Lamb
    Chopsickles, 21–22
  Melba Toast, 10
Ginger(ed)
  in Barbecue Sauce, Hoisin-Style,
    33–34
  to grate, 34
  Honey Sauce, 19–20
  Marinade for Firecracker
    Shrimp with Hot Pepper Jelly
    Glaze, 26–27
  -Soy-Citrus Marinade, Grilled
    Fish with a, 23–24
Gorgonzola, Beer-Soaked Filet
  Mignon Stuffed with, 14–15
Green Onions, Grilled, with Tequila
  Sunrise Chicken, 7–8
Grilling methods, 2
Guinness-Marinated Flank Steak
  Sandwich with Grilled Onions and
  Boursin, 15–16

H

Herb(ed)
  Butter, Mixed, 12
  Mayonnaise, 25
Hoisin-Style Barbecue Sauce, 33–34
Honey
  -Marinated Sesame Pork
    Kabobs, 19
  Sauce, Gingered, 19–20
Hot-Hot-Hot Sauce Marinade, 35

I

Indirect grilling method, 2
Italian Spice Rub, 31–32

J

Jack and Coke-Soaked
  Pork Chops, 17

K

Kabobs
  Sesame Pork,
    Honey-Marinated, 19
  Shish Kabobs, Patio Daddy-O,
    22–23

L

Lamb
  Chopsickles, 21–22
  Leg of, Red Wine-Marinated,
    with Roasted Cipollini
    Onions, 23
  Shish Kabobs, Patio Daddy-O,
    22–23
  and wine pairing, 37
Lemon
  and Garlic Marinade, for Lamb
    Chopsickles, 21–22
  Ginger-Soy-Citrus Marinade,
    Grilled Fish with a, 23–24
  and Orange Marinade, for Shish
    Kabobs, Patio Daddy-O,
    22–23
  -Pineapple Marinade, 35
  -Truffle Vinaigrette, 29
Lobster Roll, Cape Porpoise, 29

M

Marinade(s). *See also* Rub(s)
  Apple Cider Vinegar, 33
  Asian, 33
  Asian, for Pineapple Rings,
    Chinese New Year, 31
  Balsamic, for Portobello
    Burgers, 30
  Beer-Soaked Filet Mignon
    Stuffed with Gorgonzola,
    14–15
  Chipotle Chicken Thighs, 8
  Ginger, for Firecracker Shrimp
    with Hot Pepper Jelly Glaze,
    26–27
  Ginger-Soy-Citrus, Grilled Fish
    with, 23–24
  Guinness-Marinated Flank
    Steak Sandwich with Grilled
    Onions and Boursin, 15–16
  Honey-Marinated Sesame Pork
    Kabobs, 19–20
  Hot-Hot-Hot Sauce, 35
  ingredients for, 3–4
  Jack and Coke-Soaked Pork
    Chops, 17
  Lemon, for Lamb Chopsickles,
    21–22
  Orange and Lemon, for Shish
    Kabobs, Patio Daddy-O,
    22–23
  Peaches, Pickled (Liquid), Spicy
    Pork Roast with, 20
  Pineapple-Lemon Juice, 35
  Red Wine-Marinated Leg of
    Lamb with Roasted Cipollini
    Onions, 23

Salt-Cured Duck Breast with
  Fig Jam, 10–11
saltiness of, 3
Tequila, in Shrimp Margaritas
  with Avocados and Garden
  Tomatoes, 27–28
Tequila Sunrise Chicken, 7–8
Thai Flavors, Whole Fish with,
  26
Marinating
  guidelines for, 4
  in Vacu Vin Instant Marinater,
    v–vi, 1, 36
Mayonnaise, Herbed, 25
Melba Toast, Garlic, 10
Memphis in May World
  Championship Ribs, 32–33
Mop(s)
  ingredients for, 5
  Memphis in May, 32
Mushrooms
  Portobello Burgers, 30
  in Shish Kabobs, Patio Daddy-
    O, 22–23

N

Nantucket Swordfish with Browned
  Butter and Sautéed Pecans, 25–26

O

Onions
  Grilled, Guinness-Marinated
    Flank Steak Sandwich with
    Boursin and, 15–16
  Roasted Cipollini, Red Wine-
    Marinated Leg of Lamb with,
    23
  in Shish Kabobs, Patio Daddy-
    O, 22–23
Orange(s)
  Grilled, Crusty Double-Cut
    Pork Chops with, 17–18
  and Lemon Marinade, for Shish
    Kabobs, Patio Daddy-O,
    22–23
  in Tequila Sunrise Chicken, 7–8

P

Parsley, in Chimichurri Sauce,
  Cumin-Rubbed Flank Steak with,
  16
Peaches, Pickled, Spicy Pork Roast
  with, 20
Pecans, Sautéed, and Browned Butter,
  Nantucket Swordfish with, 25–26
Pepper, seasoning guidelines for, 2–3
Pepper Jelly Glaze, Hot, Firecracker
  Shrimp with, 26–27

Pernod Butter, Flat-Iron Steak with Grilled Frites and, 13–14
Pickled Peaches, Spicy Pork Roast with, 20
Pineapple
  -Lemon Juice Marinade, 35
  Rings, Chinese New Year, 31
Pork. *See also* Bacon; Ribs
  Brat Fry, Sheboygan, 20–21
  Chops, Crusty Double-Cut, with Grilled Oranges, 17–18
  Chops, Jack and Coke-Soaked, 17
  Kabobs, Sesame, Honey-Marinated, 19
  Roast, Spicy, with Pickled Peaches, 20
  Tenderloin Tacos, Smoky, 18–19
  and wine pairing, 37
Portobello Burgers, 30
Potatoes, Grilled Frites with Dijon Mustard, 14

R

Red Wine-Marinated Leg of Lamb with Roasted Cipollini Onions, 23
Renaissance Ribs, 31–32
Ribs
  Baby Back, Chinese-Take-Out, 33–34
  brining, 4
  Memphis in May World Championship, 32–33
  mopping sauce for, 5
  Renaissance, 31–32
  rubs for, 4–5
Rub(s)
  Barbecue, Classic, 33
  with Chicken, Beer-Can, The Original, 7
  Chop, Crusty Double-Cut Pork Chops with Grilled Oranges, 17–18
  Cumin, Flank Steak, -Rubbed, with Chimichurri Sauce, 16
  ingredients for, 5
  Italian Spice, 31–32
  on ribs, 4–5
  Three-Chile, in Pork Tenderloin Tacos, Smoky, 18–19

S

Salad, Chinese Five-Spice Chicken with Purple Grapes, 9–10
Salmon BLTs with Herbed Mayonnaise, 24–25
Salt
  brine formula, 4

Cured-Duck Breast with Fig Jam, 10–11
  seasoning guidelines for, 2–3
Sandwich(es)
  Burgers, Classic Backyard, 11–12
  Burgers, Portobello, 30
  Flank Steak, Guinness-Marinated, with Grilled Onions and Boursin, 15–16
  Lobster Roll, Cape Porpoise, 29
  Salmon BLTs with Herbed Mayonnaise, 24–25
Sauce(s). *See also* Butter(s)
  Anchovy-Caper, 13
  Barbecue, Hoisin-Style, 33–34
  barbecue, ingredients for, 5
  Blue Cheese Vinaigrette, 12–13
  Chimichurri, Cumin-Rubbed Flank Steak with, 16
  Honey, Gingered, 19–20
  Mop, Memphis in May, 32
  mops, about, 5
  saltiness of, 3
Scallops, Sea, Bacon-Wrapped, 28–29
Schneider, Bernd and John, 36
Seasoning guidelines, 2–3
Sesame Pork Kabobs, Honey-Marinated, 19
Sheboygan Brat Fry, 20–21
Shellfish. *See also* Fish
  Lobster Roll, Cape Porpoise, 29
  Sea Scallops, Bacon-Wrapped, 28–29
  Shrimp, Firecracker, with Hot Pepper Jelly Glaze, 26–27
  Shrimp Margaritas with Avocados and Garden Tomatoes, 27–28
  and wine pairing, 37
Shish Kabobs, Patio Daddy-O, 22–23
Shrimp
  Firecracker, with Hot Pepper Jelly Glaze, 26–27
  Margaritas with Avocados and Garden Tomatoes, 27–28
Smoky Three-Chile Rub, 19
Soy-Ginger-Citrus Marinade, Grilled Fish with a, 23–24
Spice rubs. *See* Rub(s)
Steak(s)
  Filet Mignon, Beer-Soaked, Stuffed with Gorgonzola, 14–15
  Flank, Cumin-Rubbed, with Chimichurri Sauce, 16
  Flank, Sandwich, Guinness-Marinated, with Grilled Onions and Boursin, 15–16

Flat-Iron, with Pernod Butter and Grilled Frites, 13–14
  Steakhouse-Style Cookout with à la Carte Sauces, 12–13
Steakhouse-Style Cookout with à la Carte Sauces, 12–13
Swordfish, Nantucket, with Browned Butter and Sautéed Pecans, 25–26

T

Tacos, Pork Tenderloin, Smoky, 18–19
Temperatures, for direct and indirect grilling methods, 2
Tequila
  in Shrimp Margaritas with Avocados and Garden Tomatoes, 27–28
  Sunrise Chicken, 7–8
Thai Flavors, Whole Fish with, 26
Toast, Garlic Melba, 10
Tomatoes
  Garden, and Avocados, Shrimp Margaritas with, 27–28
  Salmon BLTs with Herbed Mayonnaise, 24–25
  in Shish Kabobs, Patio Daddy-O, 22–23
Truffle-Lemon Vinaigrette, 29

V

Vacu Vin
  Champagne Saver, 38
  Instant Marinater, v–vi, 1, 36
  Rapid Ice Champagne Cooler, 38
  Rapid Ice Coolers, 38
  Wine Rack Flexible, 38
  Wine Saver, 36, 38
Veal-wine pairing, 37
Vinaigrette
  Blue Cheese, 12–13
  Lemon-Truffle, 29

W

Wine
  to cool, serve, and store, 36–38
  food pairing chart, 37
  Red Wine-Marinated Leg of Lamb with Roasted Cipollini Onions, 23
  Vaccum Wine Saver, 36

If you liked this sampler book, you'll love the complete full-sized edition of
Taming *the* Flame!

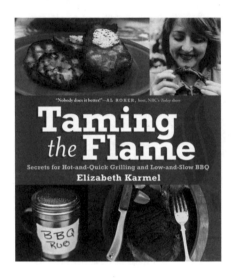

"Nobody does it better!"—Al Roker, host, NBC's *Today* show

"This authoritative, opinionated, and just plain mouth-watering book will tell you everything you need to know about barbecue from someone who's spent a lifetime walking the walk and talking the talk." —Steven Raichlen, author of *The Barbecue! Bible*

- More than 350 recipes cover everything from poultry, shellfish, beef, and sausages to ribs, Southern barbecue, fruits, and vegetables
- A special Grilling Secrets chapter reveals Karmel's signature "Grilling Trilogy" flavoring and offers the final word on basics like direct versus indirect cooking, gas versus charcoal grills, equipment, prepping and timing, and more
- 16 pages of color photographs show tantalizing dishes, and dozens of black-and-white images detail how-to techniques
- Special features include cooking time charts, practical tips, and advisory notes throughout

8 × 9 1/4 · 368 pages · 16 color photos · 78 black-and-white photos

$24.95 USA · $31.99 CAN · £15.99 UK · ISBN 0764568825